# HANDBOOK OF BIOMATERIALS & IMPLANTS

## FIRST EDITION

VISHAKHA KHAMBHATI &
DIMPAL KHAMBHATI

This book has been published with all efforts taken to make the material error-free after the consent of the author. However, the author and the publisher do not assume and hereby disclaim any liability to any party for any loss, damage, or disruption caused by errors or omissions, whether such errors or omissions result from negligence, accident, or any other cause.

While every effort has been made to avoid any mistake or omission, this publication is being sold on the condition and understanding that neither the author nor the publishers or printers would be liable in any manner to any person by reason of any mistake or omission in this publication or for any action taken or omitted to be taken or advice rendered or accepted on the basis of this work. For any defect in printing or binding the publishers will be liable only to replace the defective copy by another copy of this work then available.

Keep your dreams alive. Understand to achieve anything requires faith and belief yourself, vision, hard work, determination, and dedication. Remember all things are possible for those who believe.

This book is dedicated to my beloved parents for their endless love, support and encouragement.

*-Vishakha Khambhati*

*-Dimpal Khambhati*

# Contents

# FOREWORD

This book provides a valuable information regarding various Biomaterials and covers the necessary components used in manufacturing process of an Implants. This book is helpful for all students of Diploma as well as Degree Biomedical Engineering, Clinical science domain and material science students. If anyone wants to learn any newest trend and technologies in Material science and want to design any medical implants related to the specific material then need to understand basic concepts of material choosing criteria and manufacturing process. This book covers all those concepts that would be helpful for all the students in nearby future.

This book fully embraces the potential of the Biomaterials and Implants to empower its users. It's a friendly and approachable text intended to help you level up not just knowledge wise, but also boost up the confidence as a Biomedical Engineer for new trends in general. So dive in and get ready to learn-and welcome to the community.

-*Vishakha Khambhati*
-*Dimpal Khambhati*

# PREFACE

This book is for Biomedical Engineers, Bio-material Engineer, Material Scientists, Design Engineer and others who wants to learn about basic concepts of Biomaterials and Implants.

Our aim is to explain the enduring materialistic concepts underlying all Biological system. This book is written for a Medical developers, Biomedical Engineers, Material science Engineers and Research design Engineers.

If you study and learn the concepts in this book, you will be on your way to becoming the rare "Medical developer" who knows how things work and how to fix them. Our aim is to present the fundamental concepts in ways that you will find useful right away. You will also be prepared to studying such topics as material choosing characteristics, types of manufacturing processes, Materials handling criteria, different types of implants and risks associated with implants etc.

# Acknowledgements

A journey is easier when we travel together. This Book is the result of one year of hard work, whereby I have been accompanied and supported by many people. It is a pleasant moment that now I have an opportunity to appreciate and thank everyone, who aided in the successful completion of my book.

First, I start with my HOD and also co-author of this book, Prof. Dimpal Khambhati for providing continuous guidance and encouragement during the journey. She is a person, without whom it would be quite difficult to give shape of this book in the present format. Thanks for being an excellent guide & for guiding me on the right path. I will always be thankful to you.

Well, the word, 'Thank You' is not enough to express my feelings to my Family. The Journey was impossible, without My Parents' support, blessings, care, love and encouragement.

The last but not the least, I also thank almighty God, who blessed my life with the color of success and make me faithful to get up against any kind of stormy problems.

-*Vishakha Khambhati*
-*Dimpal Khambhati*

# Prologue

In this book the basic details of Biomaterials and related Implants is given and it is starting from the basic types of Biomaterials and designing part of specific implants.

Before learning the concepts of Biomaterials and Implants, everyone knows about some basic fundamentals of Physics and Chemistry. It has different versions can exist side by side.

By learning Biomaterials and Implants, anyone can create new trending novel implant systems.

# I

# Fundamentals of Biomaterials and Implants

## Introduction

Biomaterials are used to make devices to replace a part or a function of the body in safe, reliably economically, and physiologically acceptable manner. A variety of devices and materials are used in the treatment of disease or injury. Common place examples include suture needles, plates, teeth fillings, etc.

## *Term Definitions:*

- **Biomaterial:** A synthetic material used to make devices to replace part of a living system or to function in intimate contact with living tissue.
- **Biological Material:** A material that is produced by a biological system.
- **Bio-compatibility:** Acceptance of an artificial implant by the surrounding tissues and by the body as a whole.

# Need of Biomaterial

Biomaterial is a synthetic material used to make devices to replace part of a living system or to function in intimate contact with living tissue. In this world, now a days millions of patient suffering from tissue & organ failure mode. In order to tend patient treatment options include replacement, transplantation etc. Biomaterials are used in total hip joint replacement, shoulder joint replacement, dental implants, coronary stent, coronary catheters etc. and transplantation devices because Bio-materials are biocompatible, biodegradable, corrosion resistance, non-toxic and non-inflammatory material.

This materials are used in replacement of diseased and damaged part. Biomaterials are also used in replacement & transplantation of the living tissue & organ to improve function of the artificial body part. Biomaterials play an integral role in medicine today — restoring function and facilitating healing for people after injury or disease. Biomaterials may be natural or synthetic and are used in medical applications to support, enhance, or replace damaged tissue or a biological function. The modern field of biomaterials combines medicine, biology, physics, and chemistry, and more recent influences from tissue engineering and materials science. The field has grown significantly in the past decade due to discoveries in tissue engineering, regenerative medicine, and more.

This materials are used in replacement of diseased and damaged part. Biomaterials are also used in replacement & transplantation of the living tissue & organ to improve function of the artificial body part. Biomaterials play an integral role in medicine today — restoring function and facilitating healing for people after injury or disease. Biomaterials may be natural or synthetic and are used in medical applications to support, enhance, or replace damaged tissue or a biological function. The modern field of biomaterials combines medicine, biology, physics, and chemistry, and more recent influences from tissue engineering and materials science. The field has grown significantly in the past decade due to discoveries in tissue engineering, regenerative medicine, and more.

Biomaterial Engineers apply their knowledge of engineering and biology to design, develop and test health systems and products. Implantable devices like pacemakers, defibrillators, and artificial joints must be biocompatible while carrying out complex chemical, mechanical, and electrical functions. Metals, ceramics, plastic, glass, and even living cells and tissue all can be used in creating a biomaterial. They can be reengineered into moulded or machined parts, coatings, fibers, films, foams, and fabrics for use in biomedical products and devices. These may include heart valves, hip joint replacements, dental implants, or contact lenses. They often are biodegradable, and some are bio-absorbable, meaning they are eliminated gradually from the body after fulfilling a function.

Biomaterials are also used in aid to diagnosis and aid to treatment. These are the reasons that Biomaterials are needed in human's life.

## *Characteristics of Biomaterials:*

1. Biocompatible
2. Nontoxic
3. Non-carcinogenic
4. Good physical mechanical properties
5. Low cost
6. Moulded into different shape
7. Resistant to degradation
8. Acceptable strength
9. Resistant to wear

## *Application of Biomaterials:*

1. Orthopaedic – prosthetics used to replace joint affected by arthritis. e.g. fixation devices.
2. Cardiovascular application – artificial heart valve, stunt, etc.
3. Ophthalmology – intraocular lens and contact lens
4. Dental braces, filling, dental cap.
5. Wound healing – sutures and graft.
6. Drug delivery system – controlled and targeted delivery of drugs (doctor delivers drug to patient in remote areas).

## Classification of Biomaterial

Biomaterials have been classified into four different types: a) Metals b) Polymers c) Ceramics d) Composites.

### Metals:

- widely used for load bearing implants
- wire, screw, plates, artificial joint for hip, knee, shoulder etc.
- metal used as stainless steel, titanium and its alloy and cobalt-chromium based alloy and nitinol

### Polymers:

- Polymers resembles soft tissues and their application range from facial prosthesis to tracheal tubes, bladder, lens, tendons, etc.
- It can be used as sutures, catheters.

### Ceramics:

- Ceramics have been widely used in restorative materials in dentistry. The includes materials for crown (baby), cement, dentures (adult).

### Composites:

- The most successful composite are used in the field of dentistry as restorative material or dental cement.
- Carbon – carbon and carbon – reinforce polymer composites are used for bone repair and joint replacement because of the low elasticity modulus level.

## Construction of Biomaterial

Materials used in surgical applications such as metal, alloys, ceramics, polymers and composites that play an important role in the construction of the biomaterial. Metals, alloys, ceramics, polymers and composites are biocompatible materials. They are used to make biomedical devices. The properties of a materials are determined by its structure and chemical composition, mechanical, thermal, optical, electrical and other characterizations. Rigid metal alloys, ceramics, fibers consists of high molecular weights and that is used in bone replacement and dentistry applications.

Sherman vanadium steel was used to manufacture bone fracture plates and screws. Soft and flexible elastomers are used in soft tissue replacement. Titanium-Aluminium, Stainless steel and co-cr alloys are used in skeletal system as a high load bearing applications. Ceramics have been used for sometime in dentistry for dental crowns owing to their inertness to the body fluids, high compressive strength and good esthetic appearance. Constructing metals such as platinum, platinum-indium alloys used in stimulation of muscles, bone and nerve tissues.

Alumina is a stable and inert ceramic materials which used in orthopedic joint replacement. Some carbons also used to manufacture an implants especially for blood interfacing applications such as heart valves due to their specific strength and their biocompatibility. Polymeric materials have a variety of applications for implantation since they can be easily fabricated into many forms like fibers, textiles, films, rods and viscous fluids. Many types of polymers such as polyamides, polyethylene, polypropylene, PMMA, Polyvinylchloride are used in soft tissue of the body like skin, lens, vessel wall, chest and bladder etc. All materials consists high corrosion and wear resistance properties. Therefore above all materials are used as Biomaterials.

## Mechanical Properties of Biomaterial

For any material to be classified for biomedical application there are many requirements must be met, one of these requirement is the material should be mechanically sound; for the replacement of load bearing structures, the material should possess equivalent or greater mechanical stability to ensure high reliability of the graft.

The physical properties of ceramics depend on their microstructure, which can be characterized in terms of the number and types of phases present, the relative amount of each, and the size, shape, and orientation of each phase.

**Elastic Modulus:** Elastic modulus is simply defined as the ratio of stress to strain within the proportional limit. Physically, it represents the stiffness of a material within the elastic range when tensile or compressive load are applied. It is clinically important because it indicates the selected biomaterial has similar deformable properties with the material it is going to replace. These force-bearing materials require high elastic modulus with low deflection. As the elastic modulus of material increases fracture resistance decreases. The Elastic modulus of a material is generally calculated by bending test because deflection can be easily measured in this case as compared to very small elongation in compressive or tensile load. However, biomaterials (for bone replacement) are usually porous and the sizes of the samples are small. Therefore, the clinical test is used to determine the elastic modulus of these materials.

**Hardness:** Hardness is a measure of plastic deformation and is defined as the force per unit area of indentation or penetration. Hardness is one of the most important parameters for comparing properties of materials. Biomaterial hardness is desirable as equal to bone hardness. As above said biomaterials sample are very small therefore, micro and nano scale hardness test are used. It is rather difficult to use a traditional hardness test for ceramics and glasses due to their non-yielding nature (no plastic deformation).

**Fracture Strength:** Strength of materials is defined as the maximum stresses can be endured before fracture occurs. Strength of biomaterials (bioceramics) is important mechanical property because they are brittle in nature. A number of method are available to determine the tensile strength of material such as bending flexural test, biaxial flexural strength test, weibull approach.

**Fracture toughness:** Fracture toughness is required to alter the crack propagation in ceramics. It is help to evaluate the serviceability, performance and long term clinical success of biomaterial. It is reported that the high fracture toughness material improved clinical performance and reliability as compare to low fracture toughness.

**Fatigue:** Fatigue is defined as failure of a fabric due to repeated/cyclic loading or unloading (tensile or compressive stresses). It's additionally an necessary parameter for biomaterial because cyclic load is applied during their representing life. In this cyclic loading condition, micro crack/flaws may be produced at the interface of the matrix and the filler. This micro crack can commence permanent plastic deformation.

## Viscoelasticity

If a material exhibits Hookean elasticity, it is said to obey Hooke's law, which states that the stress applied to an elastic material will be proportional to the strain produced in it. No material is entirely elastic, but many can be modelled as such, especially if the strain is small. In a perfectly elastic material, all energy used to extend it is stored internally and released with total efficiency when it returns to its original length. The fluids for which the rate of deformation is proportional to the shear stress are called Newtonian fluids and the linear relationship for a one-dimensional system is shown in Figure.

The fluids for which the rate of deformation is proportional to the shear stress are called Newtonian fluids and the linear relationship for a one-dimensional system is shown in Figure.

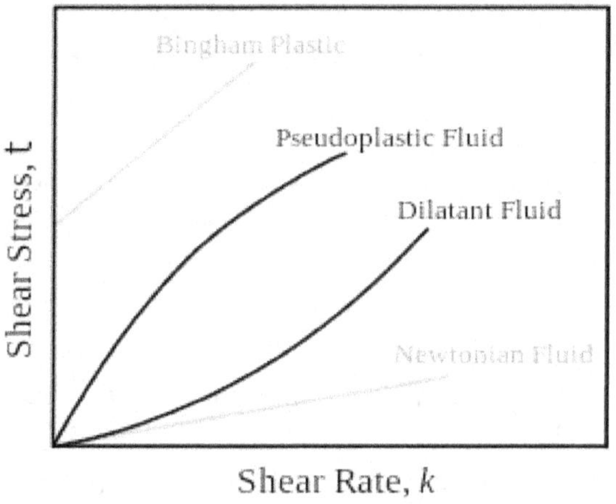


Figure 1: Variation of shear stress with rate of deformation [3]

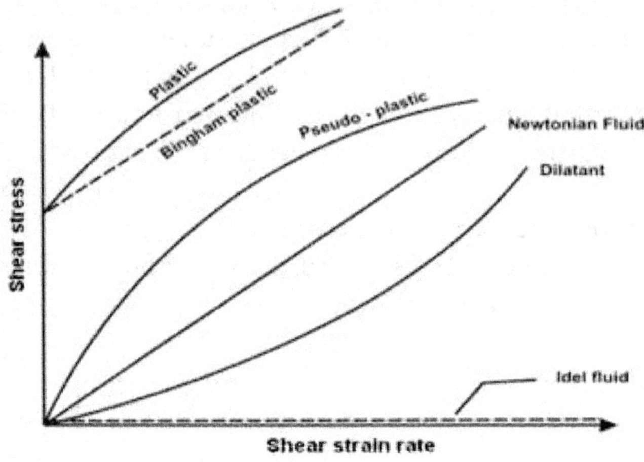


Figure 2: Variation of shear stress with rate of deformation [3]

## Wound Healing

Special processes are invoked when a material or device heals in the body. Injury to tissue will stimulate the well-defined inflammatory reaction sequence that leads to healing. When a foreign body is present in the wound site, the reaction sequence is referred to as the "foreign body reaction". This reaction will differ in intensity and duration depending upon the anatomical site involved.

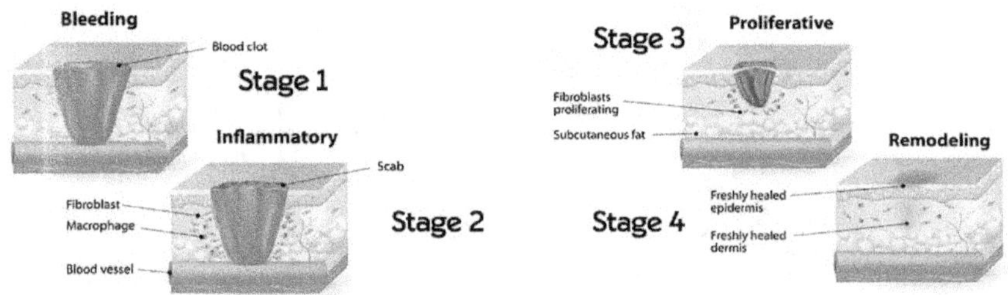


Figure 3: Phases of Wound Healing [4]

# Types of Biomaterials

The process of material selection should ideally be for a logical sequence involving:

1. Analysis of the problem
2. Consideration of requirement
3. Consideration of available material and their properties leading to
4. Choice of material

The choice of a specific biomedical material is now determined by consideration of the following:

1. A proper specification of the desired function for the material;
2. An accurate characterization of the environment in which it must function, and the effects that environment will have on the properties of the material;
3. A delineation of the length of time the material must function;
4. A clear understanding of what is meant by safe for human use.

The most common classes of materials used as biomedical materials are **polymers, metals, and ceramics.** These three classes are used singly and in combination to form most of the implantation devices available today.

## *1. Polymers:*

There are a large number of polymeric materials that have been used as implants or part of implant systems. The polymeric systems include acrylics, polyamides, polyesters, polyethylene, polysiloxanes, polyurethane, and a number of reprocessed biological materials.

Some of the applications include the use of membranes of ethylene-vinyl- acetate (EVA) copolymer for controlled release and the use of poly-glycolic acid for use as a resorbable suture material.

Some other typical biomedical polymeric materials applications include: artificial heart, kidney, liver, pancreas, bladder, bone cement, catheters, contact lenses, cornea and eye-lens replacements, external and internal ear repairs, heart valves, cardiac assist devices, implantable pumps, joint replacements, pacemaker, encapsulations, soft-tissue replacement, artificial blood vessels, artificial skin, and sutures.

As bioengineers search for designs of ever increasing capabilities to meet the needs of medical practice, polymeric materials alone and in combination with metals and ceramics are becoming increasingly incorporated into devices used in the body.

## 2. Metals:

The most commonly used implant metals are the 316L stainless steels, Ti-6%-4%V, and Cobalt base alloys. Other metal systems being investigated include Cobalt-base alloys of type "iii" and "iv", and Niobium and shape memory alloys, of which (Ti 45% - 55%Ni) is receiving most attention.

a)Iron-base alloys of the 316L stainless steel
b)Titanium and titanium-base alloys, such as
i.Ti-6% Al-4%V, and commercially pure >98.9%
ii.Ti-Ni (55% Ni and 45% Ti)
c)Cobalt base alloys of four types

## 3. Ceramics:

The most frequently used ceramic implant materials include aluminum oxides, calcium phosphates, and apatites and graphite. Glasses have also been developed for medical applications. The use of ceramics was motivated by:

- their inertness in the body,
- their formability into a variety of shapes and porosities,
- their high compressive strength, and
- their excellent wear characteristics.

Selected applications of ceramics include: hip prostheses, artificial knees, bone grafts, a variety of tissues in growth related applications in orthopedics dentistry, and heart valves. Applications of ceramics are in some cases **limited** by their generally poor mechanical properties: (a) in tension; (b) load bearing, implant devices that are to be subjected to significant tensile stresses must be designed and manufactured with great care if ceramics are to be safely used.

## *4. Composite Materials:*

Composite materials have been extensively used in dentistry and prosthesis designers are now incorporating these materials into other applications. Typically, a matrix of ultrahigh-molecular-weight polyethylene (UHMWPE) is reinforced with carbon fibers. The carbon fibers are 6-15μm in diameter. In order for the high modulus property of the reinforcing fibers to strengthen the matrix, a sufficient interfacial bond between the fiber and matrix must be achieved during the manufacturing process. This fiber reinforced composite can then be used to make a variety of implants such as intra-medullary rods and artificial joints.

## *5. Biodegradable Materials:*

Another class of materials that is receiving increased attention is biodegradable materials. Generally, when a material degrades in the body its properties change from their original values leading to altered and less desirable performance. It is possible, however, to design into an implant's performance the controlled degradation of a material, such that natural tissue replaces the prosthesis and its function. Examples include: Suture material that hold a wound together but resorb in the body as the wound heals and gains strength.

## Materials used in the body

The science of biomedical materials involves a study of the composition and properties of materials and the way in which they interact with the environment in which they are placed.

## *Fields of Knowledge to Develop Biomaterials:*

1. **Science and engineering:** (Materials Science) structure-property relationships of synthetic and biological materials including metals, ceramics, polymers, composites, tissues (blood and connective tissues), etc.
2. **Biology and Physiology:** Cell and molecular biology, anatomy, animal and human physiology, histopathology, experimental surgery,

immunology, etc.

3. **Clinical Sciences:** (All the clinical Specialties) density, maxillofacial, neurosurgery, obstetrics and gynecology, ophthalmology, orthopedics, plastic and reconstructive surgery, thoracic and cardiovascular surgery, veterinary medicine and surgery, etc.

## *Materials Evaluation:*

As the number of available materials increases, it becomes more and more important to protected the human body from unsuitable products or materials, which haven't been thoroughly evaluated.

1. **Standard Specifications:** Many standard specification tests of both national and international standards organizations (ISO) are now available, which effectively maintain quality levels. Such specifications normally give details for:
    (a) the testing of certain products,
    (b) the method of calculating the results
    (c) the minimum permissible result, which is acceptable.
2. **Laboratory Evaluation:** Laboratory tests, some of which are used in standard specification, can be used to indicate the suitability of certain materials. It is important that methods used to evaluate materials in laboratory give results, which can be correlated with clinical experience.
3. **Clinical Trials:** Although laboratory tests can provide many important and useful data on materials, the ultimate test is the controlled clinical trial and verdict of practitioners after a period of use in general practice. Many materials produce good results in the laboratory, only to be found lacking when subjected to clinical use. The majority of manufacturers carry out extensive clinical trials of new materials, normally in cooperation with a university or hospital department, prior to releasing a product for use by general practitioners.

## Impact of Biomaterials

In the early days, relatively few engineering materials such as stainless steel, chromium, etc. were used to make artificial hearts with simple design. Today field of biomaterials has evoked more than 50 different materials in various types of complex prosthetic devices. The development of biomaterials used in medical devices as occur in response to growing number of patient afflicted in traumatic and non traumatic conditions.

**Examples:**

- Arthritis – leading to joint disorder which needs correction.
- Total knee and hip replacement are achieved by using implants that are composites of metal polymer and ceramics.
- Implants which are regularly used in ophthalmology includes lens implants, corneal transplant and protective corneal shields.
- Facial implants – purely cosmetic surgery
- Oral implants is of two types: i) artificial teeth or dentures, ii) implants is totally implanted in oral cavity.
- Vascular graft are made of synthetic polymer which are routinely used to replace aorta.
- Cancer a large number of implants are used for reconstructive surgery of the breast.

## Performance of Implants

The success of a Biomaterial in the body depends on factors such as the material properties, design and biocompatibility of the material used. As well as other factors not under control of the engineer, including the technique used by the surgeon, the health and condition of the patient and the activities of the patient.

If we can assign a numerical value f to the probability of failure of an implant, then the reliability can be expressed as,

$$r = 1-f$$

If any multiple modes of failure is there then reliability is given by the product of an individual reliabilities $r_1 = (1-f_1)$ etc...

$$r_t = r_1 r_2 r_3 \ldots \ldots r_n$$

One mode of failure that can occur in biomaterial but not in engineering materials used in other contexts is an attack by the immune system on the implant. Another such failure mode is an unwanted affect of the implant up on the body. E.g. toxicity including an inflammation or causing a cancer.

Other characteristics of biomaterial that may be important in the function of an implant device made of biomaterial include adequate mechanical properties such as strength, stiffness and fatigue properties. The failure modes may differ in importance as time passes following the implant surgery. For example, consider the case of a total joint replacement in which infection is most likely seen after surgery while loosening the implant. Failure modes also depend on the type of implant, its location and function in the body. For example, an artificial blood vessel is more likely to cause problems by including a clot or becoming logged with thrombus than by breaking or tearing mechanically.

## Tissue/Body response to Implants

The term "Biocompatible" suggests that the material described good or harmonious behavior in contact with tissue and body fluids. The response of the body to implants varies widely according to the host site and species, the degree of trauma imposed during implantation and nature of implant material. Generally, the body reaction to foreign material is to reject them. The foreign material may be extruded or walled off, if it can not be removed from the body. If the material is particulate or fluid then it is ingested by the giant cells (macrophages). These process are related to the healing process of the wound where the implant is present as an additional factors.

However if the implant is inert to the tissue, then the macrophages may not be present near the implant. If the implant is chemically or physically irritating to the surrounding tissue, then inflammation occurs at the implant site. The inflammation delay normal healing process leading to the formation of granular tissue.

# II
# Metals and Ceramics

**Stainless steel**

Stainless steel is the predominant implant alloy. This is mainly due to its ease of fabrication and desirable variety of mechanical properties and corrosion behaviour. Stainless steel is least corrosion resistant suffering frequently from interface corrosion,

316L stainless steel was developed by reduction of maximum carbon content from 0.08% to 0.03% for better corrosion resistance. The chromium content of s.s. should be at least 11.0% to enable them to resist corrosion. Chromium is a reactive element. Chromium oxide on the surface of steel provides excellent corrosion resistance. Austenitic steel especially type 316 and 316L cannot be hardened by heat treatment but can be hardened by cold working. **The composition of stainless steel is given in a table:**

| Elements | 316 | 316L |
|---|---|---|
| Carbon (C) | 0.08 max | 0.03 max |
| Manganese (Mn) | 2.00 max | 2.00 max |
| Phosphorus (P) | 0.03 max | 0.03 max |
| Sulphur (S) | 0.03 max | 0.03 max |
| Silicon (Si) | 0.75 max | 0.75 max |
| Chromium (Cr) | 17.00-20.00 | 17.00-20.00 |
| Nickel (Ni) | 12.00-14.00 | 12.00-14.00 |
| Molybdenum (Mo) | 2.00-4.00 | 2.00-4.00 |

Table 1: Composition of stainless steel

Therefore ASTM recommends type 316L rather than 316 for implant fabrication. The stainless steel used in implants are generally of two types: Wrought and forged. **The mechanical properties of stainless steel is given in a table:**

| Types of Element | Elements | Ultimate tensile strength | | Yield strength | |
|---|---|---|---|---|---|
| | | Psi | MPa | Psi | MPa |
| 316 | Annealed | 75000 | 515 | 30000 | 205 |
| | Cold-Worked | 125000 | 860 | 100000 | 690 |
| 316L | Annealed | 73000 | 505 | 28000 | 195 |
| | Cold-Worked | 125000 | 860 | 100000 | 690 |

Table 2: Mechanical properties of stainless steel

The word surgical refers to that the types of steel is well suited for making surgical instrument. They are easy to clean and sterilized.

**Applications:**

1. Stainless steel are mainly used in orthopedic implants. The major uses include fracture fixation and joint replacement.

2. Hip Joints, ankle joints, knee joints, leg lengthening spacers, intramedullary rods, pins, femur shafts, bone plates, screws etc. have been developed from stainless steel.

## Cobalt-chromium based alloys

Cobalt based alloys have better corrosion in physiological environment than stainless steel. The cobalt alloys have more wear resistance than stainless steel even though they are heavier. There are basically two types:

1. Cast CoCrMo alloy (F75)
2. Wrought CoNiCrMo alloy (F562)

**Types of Co-Cr based alloys:**
ASTM lists four types of co-based alloys that are recommended for surgical implant applications:

1. **Cast CoCrMo alloy (F75)**
2. Wrought CoCrWNi alloy (F90)
3. **Wrought CoNiCrMo alloy (F562) and**
4. Wrought CoNiCrMoWFe alloy (F563)

At the present time, only two of the four alloys are used extensively in implant fabrication. **Composition of the alloys are as follows:**

| Type | ASTM Designation | Co | Cr | Mo | Ni | Fe | Si | Mn | C |
|---|---|---|---|---|---|---|---|---|---|
| Cast Co-Cr-Mo | F75 | Balance | 27-30 | 5-7 | 2.5 | 0.75 | 1.0 | 1.0 | 0.35 |
| Wrought Co-Cr-Ni-Mo | F562 | Balance | 19-21 | 9-10.5 | 33-37 | 1.0 | 0.15 | 0.15 | 0.025 |

Table 3: Composition of Cobalt-chromium based alloys

**Properties of Co-Cr based alloys:**
The two basic elements of the Co based alloys form a solid solution of upto 65 wt% Co and the remainder is Cr. The molybdenum is added to

produce finer grains, which results in higher strengths after casting and forging. Wear properties of the wrought CoNiCrMo alloys are similar to the cast CoCrMo alloy. Both cast and wrought alloys have excellent corrosion resistance. **Table shows the mechanical properties of the Co-Cr based alloys.**

| Types of Condition | Ultimate tensile strength | Yield strength |
|---|---|---|
| Cast (F75) | 655 MPa | 450 Mpa |
| Wrought (F562) Cold Worked | 1793 MPa | 1586 MPa |

Table 4: Mechanical properties of Cobalt-chromium based alloys

The modulus of elasticity for the cobalt based alloys does not change with the changes in their ultimate tensile strength. The moduli range from 220 to 234 Gpa, Which are higher than other materials such as stainless steel. The density of cobalt is 8.85 $g/cm^3$ at room temperature and young modulus is 210 $GN/m^2$.

**Applications:**

1.  Dental Implants
2.  Artificial Joints (Hip, Knee)
3.  Heavily loaded joints such as Hip Stems

# Titanium based alloys

Titanium can be alloyed with other element such as iron, aluminium, vanadium, molybdenum & others to produce strong, light weight alloy. Its low density and good mechano-chemical properties are salient features for implant applications. The major disadvantages are relatively high cost and reactivity. In several types of alloys, the most important being Ti-6%, Al-4%, Vanadium used for the production of hip prosthesis and fracture equipments.

Ti-4%, Al-6%, Vanadium used for the production of dental implant related equipments. Titanium is light metallic density 4.5 $g/cm^3$ at 25°C.

The melting point of Ti is about 1665°C. Ti-6Al-4V alloy is generally used in one of three conditions wrought, forged and cast. **Composition of the alloys are as follows:**

| Element | Composition (%) |
|---|---|
| Nitrogen (N) | 0.05% max |
| Carbon (C) | 0.08% max |
| Iron (Fe) | 0.25% max |
| Oxygen (O) | 0.18% max |
| Aluminium (Al) | 5.5-6.5% |
| Vanadium (V) | 3.5-4.5% |
| Titanium (Ti) | Remainder% |

Table 5: Composition of Titanium based alloys

**Mechanical Properties of Titanium:**

The Young's modulus of Titanium at room temperature is 107 GN/m^2, the shear modulus is 38 GN/m^2 and Poisson ratio is 0.34. Titanium alloy therefore has young's modulus of half of the stainless steel (200 GN/m^2) and cobalt-chromium alloy (200-300 GN/m^2).

The lower modulus is of significance in orthopedic devices since it offers greater flexibility. The titanium is flexible because of it have the low young modulus other than metals.

| Type | Tensile strength | Yield strength |
|---|---|---|
| Ti-Al-V | 860 MPa | 795 Mpa |

Table 6: Mechanical properties of Titanium based alloys

**Medical Applications of Titanium:**

1. The body readily accept Ti since, it is more biocompatible than stainless steel & cobalt-chromium alloys.
2. Titanium also has higher fatigue strength than any other metal.
3. Titanium has inherent properties to easily used in dental implant.
4. Titanium is a non-ferromagnetic, so patient with titanium implant can safely examine with MRI.
5. Titanium is also used for surgical instruments.
6. In most case, stainless steel is used for temporary implant and costly titanium used for permanent implant.

## Nitinol: Shape memory effect

**NITINOL,** the name represent its elemental components and the place of origin where Ni & Ti are atomic symbol for Nickel & Titanium and NOL represents Naval Ordinance Laboratory where it was discovered.

It is known for extreme flexibility & shape memory effect (SME). Nitinol is alloy of Nickel and Titanium that belongs to class of material shape memory alloy (SMA). Shape memory Nitinol has an ability to redeformed (bend at room temperature and when heated annealing returns to original shape). The alloy has three defined temperature phases: **(1) Austenite Phase (2) Martensite Phase and (3) Annealing Phase.**

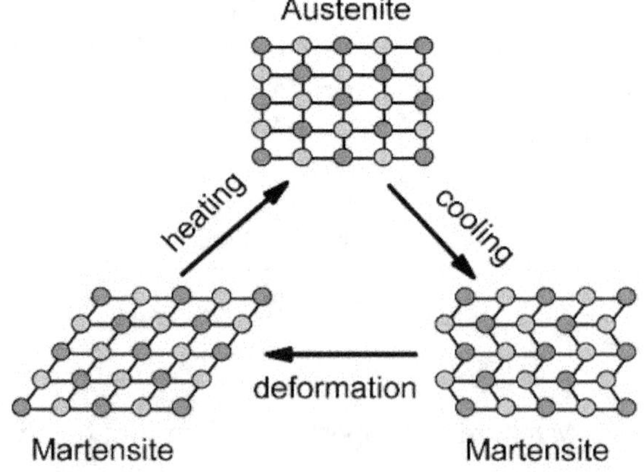


Figure 1: Temperature Phases of Nitinol alloy

**Austenite Phase:** Temperature is above transition temperature and transition temperature varies depend upon the exact composition of Nitinol alloy. Commercially, alloy usually have transitional temperature between 70-130°C.

**Martensite Phase:** It is low temperature phase, on this temperature phase alloy may be bend or deform easily.

**Annealing Phase:** In this high temperature phase, alloy will reorient with its crystalline structure to remember its parent shape.

## *Shape Memory Effect (SME):*

Nitinol has a phase change but still a solid phase. The Phase changes is known as martensite and austenite involve rearrangement of position of particle within the crystalline structure of solid. Under the transitional temperature, Nitinol is in martensite phase. In this phase, nitinol can be bend into various shape. To fix the parent shape, the metal should be held the position and heated upto 500°C. The higher temperature causes the atom to arrange themself in compact and regular pattern possible resulting in a rigid cubic arrangement. Above the transition temperature, Nitinol reverse from martensite to annealing phase with change in parent shape. **Composition & mechanical properties of the alloy are as follows:**

| Element | Composition (wt%) |
| --- | --- |
| Ni | 54.01 |
| Co | 0.64 |
| Cr | 0.76 |
| Mn | 0.64 |
| Fe | 0.66 |
| Ti | Balance |

Table 7: Composition of Nitinol alloy

| Melting Point | 1240° C to 1310° C |
|---|---|
| Density | 6.59 g/cm^3 |
| Tensile strength | 2,00,000 PSI |
| Resistance | 125 Ω/inch |

Table 8: Mechanical properties of Nitinol alloy

**Application & Property of Nitinol:**

1. **Thermal shape memory:** It is more popular for reusable, medical instrument. Surgeon can shape device on site to fit a patients geometry than after heat sterilization the device return to its original shape for next procedure. **Application:** Heart valve tools
2. **Flexibility:** It allows it to be bend more significantly than stainless steel. **Application:** Guided wire
3. **Constancy of stress:** Nitinol arch wire move with the teeth applying a constant force over a broad treatment time and position. **Application:** Orthodontic arch wire
4. **Elastic spring back:** That can return to its original shape after removing the stress. **Application:** Biopcy marker
5. **Biocompatibility:** It is less corrosive than stainless steel. **Application:** Implants

Nitinol has been extensively used in dentistry because of its resilience and shape memory property. Devices made from the alloy include flexible wire clasps, pre-stretched wire and band or double wedge materials for rapid wedging or separation of teeth.

## Ceramics and its types

Ceramic is defined as "Synthesized inorganic solid, crystalline materials, excluding metals." Ceramics used as biomaterials to fill defects in tooth and bone to fix bone grafts, fracture or prosthesis to bone and to replace diseased tissue are called Bio ceramics. They must be highly biocompatible and antithrombogenic and should not be toxic, allergenic, carcinogenic or teratogenic.

Bioceramics can be classified into three groups:

1. **Bio-Inert Ceramics (Inert/Non-absorbable ceramics):** Alumina, Zirconia, carbons
2. **Bio-Active Ceramics (Surface Reactive/Semi-Inert ceramics):** HAP (Hydroxyapatite), Glass Ceramics (Bio-glass and Ceravital)
3. **Bio-Resorbable Ceramics (Bio-Degradable/Non-Inert):** Calcium-Phosphate

Ceramics show numerous applications as biomaterials due to their physical-chemical properties. They have the advantage of being inert in the human body, and their hardness and resistance to abrasion makes them useful for bones and teeth replacement.

1. **Bio-inert ceramics** have a high chemical stability in vivo as well as high mechanical strength as a rule, and when they are implanted in living bone, they are incorporated into the bone tissue in accordance with the pattern of "Contact osteogenesis".
2. **Bio-active ceramics** have the capability of chemical bonding with living bone tissue. In other words, When bio-active ceramics are implanted in living bone, they are incorporated into the bone tissue in accordance with the pattern of "bonding osteogenesis". The mechanical strength of Bio-active ceramics is generally lower than the Bio-inert ceramics.
3. **Bio-resorbable ceramics** are gradually absorbed in vivo and replaced by bone in the bone tissue. The pattern of their incorporation into the bone tissue is considered similar to contact osteogenesis, although the interface between bio-resorbable ceramics and bone is not stable as that observed with bioinert ceramics.

The most frequently used ceramic implant materials include aluminium oxides, calcium phosphates, apatite and graphite. Glasses have also been developed for medical applications. The use of ceramics was motivated by:

- Their inertness in the body
- Their formability into a variety of shapes
- Their high compressive strength

- Their excellent wear characteristics

Selected applications of ceramics include,

1. Hip prosthesis
2. Artificial Knee
3. A variety of tissue growth related applications like Orthopedic, Dentistry and Heart Valves.

Applications of ceramics are in some cases limited by their poor mechanical properties like in tension and load bearing.

## *Alumina as a Bio-inert ceramics*

Inert means materials that are essentially stable with little or no tissue reactivity when implanted within the living organisms. When a Biomaterial is nearly inert & the interface is not chemically or biologically bonded, there is relative movement & progressive development of a Non-adherent fibrous capsule in soft and hard tissues.

So the movement of the biomaterial tissue interface eventually leads to deterioration of the implant. High density, High purity (>99.5%) Alumina was the first bio-ceramic widely used.

It is used in load-bearing hip prosthesis & dental implants because of excellent corrosion resistance, good biocompatibility, high wear resistance & high strength. Most Alumina devices are very fine grained polycrystalline $\alpha$-Al2O3. A very small amount of magnesia is used to sintering & to limit grain growth during sintering. Alumina with an average grain size of <4µm & >99.7% purity exhibits good flexural strength & excellent compressive strength.

**Advantages:**

1. High Density, High Purity (>99.5%)
2. Excellent corrosion resistance
3. Good Bio-compatibility
4. High Wear Resistance
5. High Strength & Good Flexural strength
6. Excellent Compressive strength

| Material | Young's Modulus | Compressive strength | Hardness | Density (g/cm^3) |
|---|---|---|---|---|
| $Al_2O_3$ | 380 GPa | 400 MPa | 2000-3000 | >3.9 |

Table 9: Mechanical properties of Alumina

**Applications:**

1. Knee Prosthesis
2. Bone Screws
3. Jaw Bone Reconstruction
4. Segmental Bone Replacement
5. Blade, Screws or Post Dental Implant
6. HIP-PROSTHESIS (Ball made up of Alumina & Socket components made of UHMWPE- Ultra High Molecular Weight Polyethylene

## *Bioglass as a Bio-active Ceramics*

**Bioactive ceramics:** Bioactive ceramics are as material with an interfacial response that results in tissue bonding. Thus, it refers to a material that has been designed to induce "Specific biological activity" or "bone bonding".

The Objective of this type of implant material is to achieve a controlled surface reactivity that will induce a direct chemical bond between the implant and the surrounding tissues. Bioglass and ceravital are two glass ceramics having fine grained structure with excellent mechanical and thermal properties, which are used in implants. Al2O3, TiO2 & Ta2O3 are present in ceravital in order to control the dissolution rate of the ceramic.

**Properties of Glass ceramics:**

1. It is composed of glasses and ceramics. The thermal coefficient of expansion is very low, typically 10^-7 to 10^-5 degree C.
2. Tensile strength is about 100 MPa to 200 MPa.
3. Resistance to scratching and abrasion is close to the sapphire.

**Limitations:**

1. Brittle in nature.
2. Easily deform.

**Applications:**

1. Used in Dental Implants as a Filler material.
2. Used in Bone cement, dental restorative material and as a coating material.

## *Calcium Phosphate as a Bioresorbable Ceramics*

**Bioresorbable ceramics:** Bioresorbable ceramics are gradually absorbed in vivo and replaced by bone in the bone tissue. The pattern of their incorporation into the bone tissue is considered similar to contact osteogenesis, although the interface between bioresorbable ceramics and bone is not stable as that observed with bio inert ceramics.

**Use of Bioresorbable ceramics:**

1. As drug delivery devices
2. For repairing bone damaged due to disease or trauma
3. For filling space vacated by bone screws, donor bone, excised tumors and diseased bone loss
4. For repairing and fusion of spinal and lumbo-sacral vertebra
5. For repairing herniated disc
6. For repairing maxillofacial, dental defects and ocular implant

**Calcium Phosphate:** One of the first resorbable implant substances used was plaster of Paris. Calcium phosphate has been used in the form of artificial bone. Recently, this material has been used for manufacturing various forms of implants as well as for solid or porous coatings on other implants.

Two types of orthophosphoric acid salt TCP (Tricalcium phosphate) & HAP (Hydroxyapatite) used as resorbable biomaterials. Calcium phosphate can be crystallized into salts hydroxyapatite and β-whitlockite will be formed. Both forms are very tissue compatible and are used for bone substitute in a granular form as a solid block. The mineral part of bone and teeth, is made of a crystalline form of calcium phosphate similar to hydroxyapatite. The ideal Ca:P ratio of HAP is 10:6 and calculated density is 3.219 g/cm3. **Properties of Hydroxyapatite is as follows:**

| Property | Value |
| --- | --- |
| Elastic modulus | 40-117 GPa |
| Compressive strength | 294 MPa |
| Bending strength | 147 MPa |
| Hardness | 3.43 GPa |
| Poisson's ratio | 0.27 |
| Density | 3.16 g/cm3 |

Table 10: Physical properties of Hydroxyapatite

Polycrystalline hydroxyapatite has a high elastic modulus. Hydroxyapatite having an excellent Biocompatibility. Drawback of calcium phosphate ceramics is their rather complicated fabrication process and particularly difficult shaping.

## Carbons

**Carbons:** Carbons is a versatile element and exists in a variety of forms. Carbons is mostly used in orthopaedic Implants unlike Metals, Polymers & other ceramics, these carbonaceous materials do not suffer from Fatigue. Their intrinsic brittleness & low tensile strength limits their use in major load bearing applications. It is used as biomaterial particularly in contact with blood.

Mitral & aortic valve constructed by pyrolytic carbon. It does not corrode & is also an efficient electrical conductor in vivo.

**Types of carbons:** Carbon, Carbon fiber, Pyrolitic carbon, Vapour grown carbon

| Material | Young's Modulus | Compressive strength | Hardness | Density (g/cm^3) |
|---|---|---|---|---|
| Pyrolitic Carbon | 17-28 | 900 MPa | NA | 1.7-2.2 |
| Vitreous Carbon | 24-31 | 172 MPa | 150-200 | 1.4-1.6 |

Table 11: Mechanical properties of Carbons

## Dentals Metals: Gold

**Gold:** Gold and gold alloys have good durability, corrosion resistance and stability which makes them useful for dentistry. There are two methods for gold fillings: melting and casting.

Gold alloys are used for cast restoration, as they have more mechanical properties than pure gold. Copper, filled with gold, significantly increases its strength.

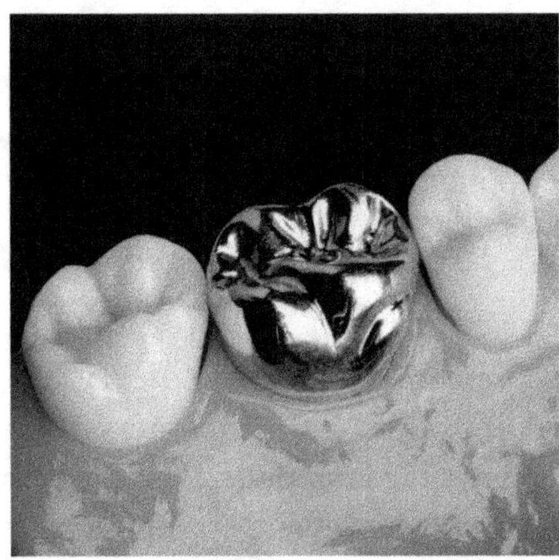

Figure 2: Gold metal used in dentistry application

## Corrosion of Metals

Corrosion is an undesirable chemical reaction of a metal with its environment, resulting in continuous degradation of oxides, hydroxides or other compounds. Human body presents a very aggressive environment to the metals used for implanting (Oxygen, body fluids). Corrosion resistance of metallic implant material is an important aspect of its biocompatibility as a result. The reaction of metals with an aqueous atmosphere is electrochemical in nature involving the motion of electrons in the cathode. For metals implanted in an aqueous atmosphere with dissolved oxygen, the primary anodic and cathode reactions are occurred.

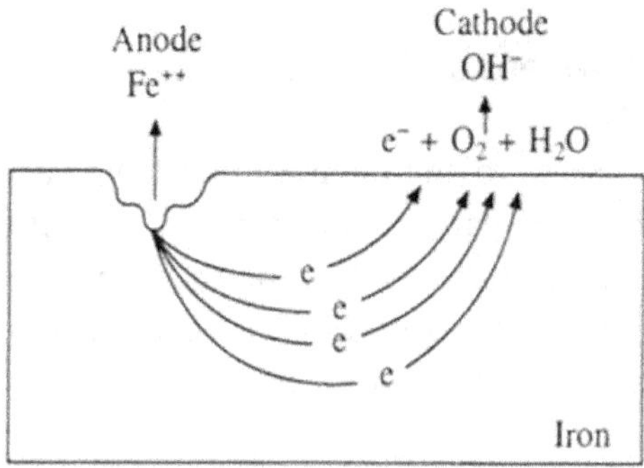


Figure 3: Corrosion of metals

The crevices between components, wounds etc., can have extremely low oxygen concentrations leading to cathodic reduction of water as given in equation:

$$M \rightarrow M^{n+} + ne^-$$
$$2H_2O + 2e^- \rightarrow H_2 + 2OH^-$$

Most of the corrosion in metals is caused by the oxidation process at the anode. Corrosion can be accelerated in the presence of static or dynamic stresses.

**Passivation** - Materials have their corrosion resistance due to the formation of oxide or compact solid films of hydroxides on the surface. For example, the high chemical durability of stainless steel is due to the chromium oxide film on the surface.

**Pitting or fretting corrosion** - If the passivation film is broken, corrosion occurs at the point where it becomes anodic, while the rest of the material becomes cathodic.

Alternatively, implant failure may occur due to a mechanical incompatibility between the device and the body. The implanting material used today is much harder than bone, so that the distribution of stress in the bone is set. Implantation loosening can result from improper stress distribution.

## Manufacturing Process of Biomaterials

Manufacturing processes create finished goods from various raw materials. Manufacturing processes can be in terms of primary and secondary processes, where primary processes are used in creating basic forms and secondary processes are used to alter or add features to these forms.

1. Metal deformation
2. Metal casting
3. Sheet metal forming
4. Polymer processing
5. Machining
6. Finishing
7. Assembly

**Metal deformation:** Metal deformation is used to transform bulk materials in the form of billets, blooms, and slabs as they come from a mill into other shapes such as pipe or bars. Extrusion is one such process, where ductile metals such as copper and aluminium are forced through dies to produce common shapes such as copper tubing or aluminium angles. Tubing manufacturing typically uses a mandrel in addition to a die to produce a hollow cross-section.

Forging uses hydraulic die sets or open dies and hammers to plastically deform usually hot metal into net shapes, oftentimes starting with a rough approximation of the finished shape called a blocked preform.

**Casting:** Casting creates complex shapes from molten metal. Sand casting creates a two-piece sand mold around a pattern. After the pour, the metal cools and solidifies, following which the mold is broken away to reveal the finished casting.

Die casting uses permanent molds into which low melt point metals such as zinc are injected under pressure. Investment casting creates intricate wax patterns that are coated with slurry, the wax melted out, then filled with molten metal.

**Sheet metal forming:** Sheet metal operations can be grouped as shearing, blanking, drawing, punching, embossing, and bending. Sheet metal is cut into smaller straight-edged pieces by shearing. Drawing gradually pushes the material into a die cavity that deepens with each step through the die. Punching creates holes and slots where needed. Bending creates tabs and other features that run perpendicular to the plane of the original material. Blanking shears the finished part from the remaining coil material that has served to carry the forming part through the die.

**Polymer processing:** Polymer processing involves the forming of both thermoset and thermoplastic materials usually by molding but also by subtractive methods such as machining. Of the various molding methods, compression, blow, and injection molding are the most common.

In compression molding, an elastomer charge is placed between heated die halves which are subsequently closed to force the material into the shape of the cavity. Transfer molding is another compression molding technique in which the heated polymer is injected into the closed mold. Blow molding is a common method for making plastic bottles. Here, a softened parison is filled with air to force it against the walls of the closed mold halves. Injection molding uses an auger to soften plastic pellets in a barrel and inject the resulting "shot" under high pressure into a usually multi-cavity mold.

Thermoforming is another polymer processing method that shapes sheets or films of thermoplastic into cavities or over plugs usually using vacuum or air to pull or push the softened material against the mold surfaces.

**Machining:** Machining uses various cutting tools, abrasive wheels, as well as some unusual media such as water or sparks, to remove material from round and bar stock, castings, etc. to produce accurate finished goods. Machining methods include sawing, turning, boring, reaming, etc. and are oftentimes performed as secondary operations to clean up parts or to create surfaces that are suitable for assembly.

**Finishing:** Finishing encompasses many final operations that make a part ready for assembly. Finishing steps occur after assembly as well, such as post-weld heat treating.

**Assembling:** Assembly is where the different parts that compose a finished product come together. Various forms of fastening are often used, including mechanical forms such as screws and rivets, fusion methods such as welding, bonding techniques and interference methods such as press and shrink fitting.

# III

# Polymers

## Introduction

Polymers (from the Greek: polys, many; meros, part or unit) are large molecules made up by the repetition of small, simple chemical units termed **monomers.** In some cases the repetition appears much as a chain is built up from its links. In other cases the chains are branched are interconnected to form three-dimensional networks.

Polymers have found applications in every specialty area and continue to be the most widely used materials in health care. Polymers can be classified in several different ways according to their structures, the type of reactions by which they are prepared, their physical properties, or their technological use.

The following factors influence the mechanical properties of polymers:

**1. Composition 2. Molecular weight 3. Amount of unreacted monomer in the polymer 4. Morphology 5. Crystallinity 6. Configurational structure 7. Additives.**

Synthetic polymeric materials have been widely used in medical disposable supplies, prosthetic materials, dental materials, implants, dressings, extracorporeal devices, encapsulants, polymeric drug delivery systems, tissue engineered products. The main advantages of the polymeric biomaterials compared to metal or ceramic materials are ease of manufacturability to produce various shapes (latex, film, sheet, fibers, etc.), ease of secondary processability, reasonable cost, and availability with desired mechanical and physical properties.

## Polymerization

The required properties of polymeric biomaterials are similar to other biomaterials, that is, biocompatibility, sterilizability, adequate mechanical and physical properties, and manufacturability. The Number of repeating units in chain formed in polymer is known as the **degree of polymerization.**

In order to link the small molecules one has to force them to lose their electrons by the chemical process of **condensation and addition.** By controlling the reaction temperature, Pressure and time in the presence of catalyst, the degree to which repeating units are put together into chains can be manipulated.

## *Condensation (step reaction) Polymerization:*

**Condensation or step reaction polymerization:** During condensation polymerization, a small molecule such as water will be condensed out by the chemical reaction for e.g.

$$R\text{-}NH_2 + R'COOH \rightarrow R'CONHR + H_2O$$

$$(\text{amine}) \quad (\text{carboxylic acid}) \quad\quad (\text{amide}) \quad\quad (\text{condensed molecule})$$

This Particular process is used to make Polyamides (Nylons). Nylon was the first commercial polymer, made in the 1930s. One major drawback of condensation polymerization is the tendency for the reaction to cease before the chains grow to a sufficient length. This is due to the decreased mobility of the chains and reactant chemical species as polymerization progresses.

This results in short chains. However, in the case of nylon the chains ar polymerized to a sufficiently large extent before this occurs and the physical properties of the polymer are preserved. Natural polymers, such as polysaccharides and proteins, are also made by condensation polymerization. The condensing molecule is always water (H2O).

## *Addition (free radical) Polymerization:*

Addition polymerization can be achieved by rearranging the bonds within each monomer. Since each "mer" has to share at least two covalent electrons with other mers the monomer should have at least one double bond. For example, in the case of ethylene:

$$n \begin{Bmatrix} H & H \\ | & | \\ C = C \\ | & | \\ H & H \end{Bmatrix} \rightarrow \begin{matrix} H & H & H & H \\ | & | & | & | \\ -C + C - C + C- \\ | & | & | & | \\ H & H & H & H \end{matrix}$$

The breaking of a double bond can be done with an initiator. This is usually a free radical such as benzoyl peroxide ($C_6H_5COO-OOCC_6H_5$). The initiation can be activated by heat, ultraviolet light, and other chemicals. The free radicals (initiators) can react with monomers and this free radical can react with another monomer and the process can continue on. This process is called propagation. The propagation process can be terminated by combining two free radicals, by transfer, or by disproportionate processes. There are three more types of initiating species for addition polymerization besides free radicals: cations, anions, and coordination (stereospecific) catalysts.

E.g.

1. Ethylene $CH_2=CH_2$
2. Propylene $CH_2=CH-CH_3$
3. Styrene $CH_2=CH-C_6H_5$

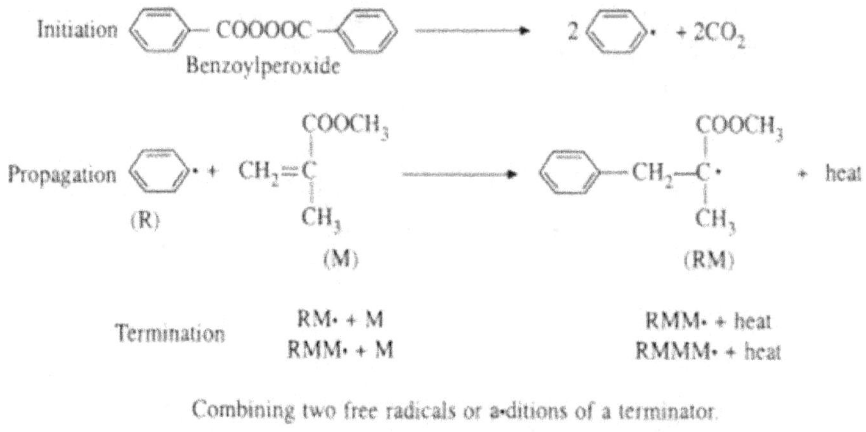

Figure 1: Addition Polymerization

## Polymer Chain

The propagation process can be terminated by combining two free radicals, by transfer, or by disproportionate processes. The degree of polymerization (DP) is defined as an average number of mers, or repeating units, per chain. The polymer chains can be arranged in linear, branched & cross-linked or three dimensional network forms depending upon the degree of polymerization.

The relation between molecular weight (M and DP) can be expressed by equation:

$$M = DP \times MW \text{ of Monomer}$$

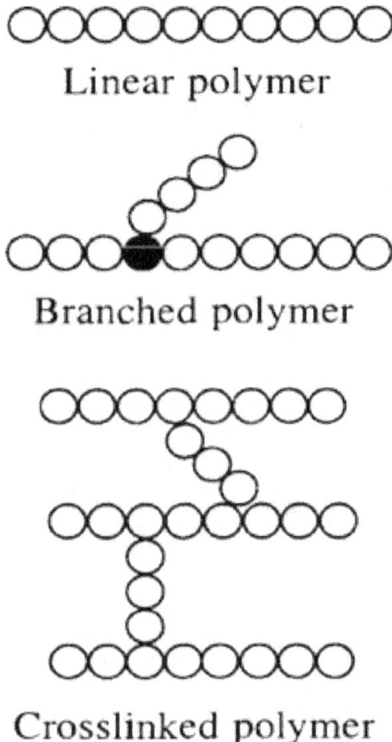


Figure 2: Polymer Chain

As the molecular chains become longer by the progress of polymerization, their relative mobility decreases. The chain mobility is also related to the physical properties of the final polymer. Generally, the higher the molecular weight, the less the mobility of chains which results in higher strength and greater thermal stability. The polymer chains can be arranged in three ways; linear, branched, and a cross-linked (or three-dimensional) network.

Linear polymers such as polyvinyls, polyamides, and polyesters are much easier to crystallize than the cross-linked or branched polymers. However, they cannot be crystallized 100% as with metals. Instead they become semicrystalline polymers. The arrangement of chains in crystalline regions is believed to be a combination of folded and extended chains. The chain folds, which are seemingly more difficult to form. Copolymerization, in which two or more homopolymers (one type of repeating unit throughout its structure) are chemically combined, always disrupts the regularity of polymer chains thus promoting the formation of a noncrystalline structure.

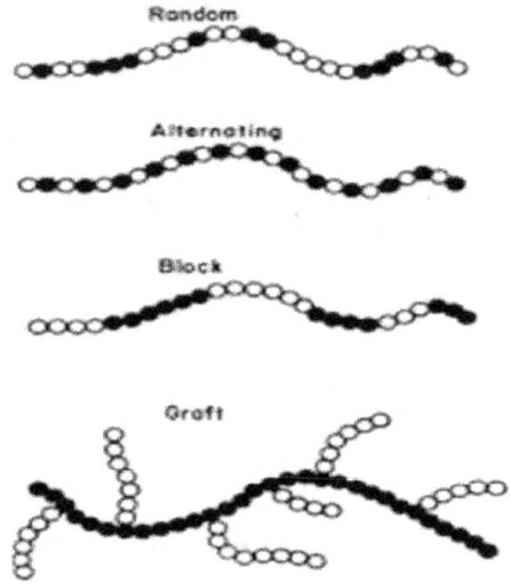


Figure 3: Different types of polymer chain

Elastomers, or rubbers, are polymers which exhibit large stretchability at room temperature and can snap back to their original dimensions when the load is released. The elastomers are non-crystalline polymers which have an intermediate structure consisting of long chain molecules in three-dimensional networks. The chains also have "kinks" or "bends" in them which straighten when a load is applied.

## Polymers in biomedical use

The structures of polymers determine their utilization in various medical domains. Their selection for subsequent employment in surgery, dermatology, ophthalmology, pharmacy, etc. is mainly determined by their chemical and physical properties.

However, the stability and lifetime of polymers in long-term implantation depend not only on chemical structure of the material employed but also on the conditions under which they are utilized. The same material may have different characteristics depending on its utilization.

Biomedical polymers can be classified into either **elastomers or plastics. Elastomers** are able to withstand large deformations and return to their original dimensions after releasing the stretching force. **Plastics** on the other hand are more rigid materials and can be classified into two types: **thermoplastic and thermosetting.**

**Thermoplastic polymers** can be melted, reshaped and reformed. The **thermosetting plastics** cannot be remelted and reused, since the chemical reactions that have taken place are irreversible.

The **thermoplastic polymers** used as biomaterials include polyolefins, Teflon®(fluorinated hydrocarbons), poly (methyl methacrylate) (PMMA), poly (hydroxyethyl methyacrylate) (PHEMA, Hydron®), polyvinyl chloride (PVC), polycarbonate, nylon, polyester (Dacron®) etc.

An example of **thermosetting plastic** is the epoxy resin cross-linked with a curing agent. A number of elastomers have been tried as implant materials. These include, butyl rubber, chlorosulfonated polyethylene (Hypalon®), epichlorohydrin rubber (Hydrin®), polyurethane (Biomer®, Pellethane®, Texin®, Tecoflex HR®, Lyca T-126®), natural rubber and silicone rubber (Silastic®).

## Types of Polymer

Polymers have assumed an important role in medical applications. In most of these applications, Polymers have little or no competition from other types of materials. Their unique properties are:

1. Flexibility
2. Resistance to biochemical attack
3. Good Biocompatibility
4. Light weight
5. Available in a wide variety of compositions with adequate physical and mechanical properties
6. Can be easily manufactured into products with the desired shape.

Applications in Biomedical field as:

1. Tissue Engineering
2. Implantation of medical devices and artificial organs due to its inert nature

3.  Prosthesis
4.  Dentistry
5.  Bone repair
6.  Drug delivery and targeting into sites of inflammation or tumors
7.  Plastic tubing for intra-venous infusion
8.  Bags for the transport of blood plasma
9.  Catheter

Types of Polymers are as follows:

1.  Polyethylene
2.  Polypropylene
3.  Per-fluorinated polymers
4.  Acrylic polymers
5.  Polyamides
6.  Poly Methyl Methacrylate (PMMA)
7.  Silicone Rubber
8.  Prosthodontics polymer

## I. Polyethylene (PE):

It is chemically the simplest of all polymers and as a homochain polymer. Polyethylene (PE) and their copolymers are called Polyolefins. These are linear thermoplastics. PE is available commercially in three major grades:

$$\left(\!\!\begin{array}{ccc} H & & H \\ | & & | \\ C & \!\!-\!\! & C \\ | & & | \\ H & & H \end{array}\!\!\right)_{n}$$

1.  High Density (HDPE)
2.  Low Density (LDPE)

3. Ultra high molecular weight (UHMWPE)

**It is essentially:**

1. Stable and suitable for long time implantation under many circumstances
2. Relatively inexpensive
3. Has good general mechanical properties

So that it has become a versatile biomedical polymer with applications ranging from catheters to joint replacement.

**Uses:**

1. Tubes for various catheters
2. Hip Joint
3. Knee Joint Prosthesis
4. Pharmaceutical bottles

The first PE was synthesized by reacting ethylene gas at high pressure (100-300 Mpa) in the presence of a catalyst (peroxide) to initiate polymerization. The process yields the low density polyethylene (LDPE). By using a ziegler catalyst, HDPE can be produced at low pressure (10 Mpa). The crystalinity, density are increases due to the result is better packing of the chains.

**Properties:**

1. Low cost
2. Easy Processibility
3. Excellent Electrical Insulation Properties
4. Excellent chemical resistance
5. Toughness and flexibility even at low temperature

Some important physical properties of PE are given in table:

| Property | LDPE | HDPE | UHMWPE |
|---|---|---|---|
| Density (g/cm^3) | 0.90-0.92 | 0.92-0.96 | 0.93-0.94 |
| Tensile Strength (Mpa) | 7.6 | 23-40 | 27 |
| Elongation (%) | 150 | 400-500 | 200-250 |
| Modulus of Elasticity (Mpa) | 96-260 | 410-1240 | 1100-2000 |
| Crystallinity (%) | 50-70 | 70-80 | 80-95 |

Table 1: Physical properties of Polyethylene

The UHMWPE has been used extensively for orthopedic implant fabrications, especially for load bearing surfaces such as Total hip and Knee joints. HDPE is used in pharmaceutical bottles, non-woven fabrics and cups. LDPE is used in tubes for various catheters.

## II. Polypropylene (PP):

Its chemical structure is as follows. There are three types depending on the position of the methyl (CH3) group along with the polymer chain.

$$(C_3H_6)_n$$

It has several properties like:

- Excellent chemical resistance
- Weak permeability to water vapours
- Good transparency
- Good surface reflection

Polypropylene (PP) is widely used in medical devices like sutures, artificial vascular grafts, blood oxygenator membrane, packaging for devices etc. Another uses of Polypropylene are:

1. Yarn for surgery
2. Sutures
3. Disposable hypothermic syringe
4. Blood oxygenator membrane
5. Artificial vascular grafts
6. Finger joint prosthesis

Polypropylene (PP) can be synthesized using a ziegler type catalyst that controls the position of each side group as it is being polymerized to allow the formation of a regular chain structure from the asymmetric repeating unit.

There are three types of structure can exist depending upon the position of the methyl (CH3) group along the polymer chain. The random distribution of methyl group in the atactic polymer prevents close packing of chains abd results in amorphous polypropylene. The isotactic and syndiotactic structures have a regular position of the methyl side groups in the same side and alternate side respectively. They usually crystallize.

**Specific Properties of PP:**

- Excellent chemical resistance
- Weak permeability to water vapour
- Good transparency
- Good surface reflection

**Physical properties of Polypropylene (PP):**

| Property | Value |
| --- | --- |
| Density (g/cm^3) | 0.90-0.91 |
| Tensile Strength (Mpa) | 28-36 |
| Elongation (%) | 400-900 |
| Modulus of Elasticity (Mpa) | 1.1-1.55 |

Table 2: Physical properties of Polypropylene

## III. Per-Fluorinated Polymer (PTFE):

Per-fluorinated polymer is also known as Polytetrafluoroethylene (PTFE). PTFE is a fluorocarbon based polymer. Commercially, the material is best known as Teflon. It is made by free-radical polymerization of tetrafluoroethylene and has a carbon back bone chain where each carbon has two fluorine atoms attached to it.

$$\left(\begin{array}{cc} F & F \\ | & | \\ C - C \\ | & | \\ F & F \end{array}\right)_n$$

**Properties:**

1.  Hydrophobic (Water hating)
2.  Biologically inert
3.  Non biodegradable
4.  Has low friction characteristics
5.  Relatively lower wear resistance

6. Highly crystalline (94%)
7. Very high density, Low modulus of elasticity
8. Low tensile strength

**Uses:**

1. Artificial grafts (artificial vascular graft)
2. Catheter
3. Sutures
4. Uses in reconstructive and cosmetic facial surgery

**Disadvantages of PTFE:**

PTFE has relatively low wear resistance. Under composition or in solutions where rubbing or abrasion can occur, it can produce wear particles. These can result in a chronic inflammatory reaction, an undesirable outcome.

## IV. Polyamide (Nylons):

Polyamides are known as Nylons and are designed by the number of carbon atoms in the repeating units. The basic chemical structure of the repeating unit of polyamides can be written into two ways:

$$\left(\!\!-\overset{\overset{\displaystyle H}{|}}{N}-(CH_2)_6-\overset{\overset{\displaystyle H}{|}}{N}-\overset{\overset{\displaystyle O}{||}}{C}-(CH_2)_4-\overset{\overset{\displaystyle O}{||}}{C}\!-\!\right)_{\!n}$$

**Nylon 66**

$$\left(\!\!-\overset{\overset{\displaystyle H}{|}}{N}-(CH_2)_5-\overset{\overset{\displaystyle O}{||}}{C}\!-\!\right)_{\!n}$$

**Nylon 6**

Equation (i) represents polymers made from diamine and diacids such as type 66 (x=6, y=4) and 610 (x=6, y=8) and equation (ii) represents the nylon 6 (x=5) and nylon 11 (x=10) etc.

Nylons can be polymerized by step reaction and ring scission polymerization. They have excellent fiber-forming ability due to interaction hydrogen bonding and a high degree of crystallinity, which increases strength in the fiber direction. The presence of –CONH– groups in the polyamide attracts the chain strongly toward one another by hydrogen bonding. It provide physical properties such as strength: Nylon 66 is stronger than Nylon 610 and Nylon 6 is stronger than Nylon 11.

**Physical properties of Polyamides (Nylons):**

| Property | Nylon Types | | | |
|---|---|---|---|---|
| | 66 | 610 | 6 | 11 |
| Density (g/cm^3) | 1.14 | 1.09 | 1.13 | 1.05 |
| Tensile Strength (Mpa) | 76 | 55 | 83 | 59 |
| Elongation (%) | 90 | 100 | 300 | 120 |
| Modulus of Elasticity (Mpa) | 2.8 | 1.8 | 2.1 | 1.2 |

Table 3: Physical properties of Polyamide (Nylons)

**Specific properties of Polyamides (Nylons):**

1. Very good mechanical property
2. Resistance to abrasion & breaking
3. Stability to shock & fatigue
4. Low friction co-efficient
5. Good thermal properties
6. Good chemical resistance
7. Permeable to gases

**Applications of Polyamides (Nylons):**

Nylon tubes find applications in intra cardiac catheters. They are utilized as components of dialysis devices. The coated nylon sutures find wide biomedical applications.

## *V. Acrylic Polymers:*

Simple acrylates have relatively high toughness and strength. These are obtained through addition polymerization of acrylic acid derivatives. The most widely used poly acrylate is poly (methyl methacrylate, PMMA). It is somewhat brittle in comparison with other polymers. It has an excellent light transparency (> 92% transmission) and a high index of refraction (1.49).

This transparent material is sometimes referred as organic glass. It has excellent chemical resistivity and is highly biocompatible in the pure form. Therefore, this polymer is used extensively in medico-surgical applications as contact lenses, implantable ocular lenses, bone cement for joint fixation, dentures and maxillofacial prostheses. Acrylic resins can be cast molded or machined with conventional tools.

They can be formed into the desired shape by thermoplastic means such as injection molding or in a chemoplastic way, i.e. curing a mixture of polymer and monomer in a mold at elevated temperatures. Most medical and dental acrylic resins are available as a two component system: a powder, which consists mainly of small poly (methyl methacrylate) spheres and beads and a liquid, containing the monomer. The powder and liquid are mixed in a ratio of approximately 2: 1 w/w and an easily moldable dough is obtained which cures in about 10 min or more quickly after heating in a gypsum mold.

The monomer polymerizes and binds together the preexisting polymer particles. For dental purpose, pigments and fillers can be added to the powder. Surgical bone cements contain barium sulfate or zirconium oxide. Chemical Structure of Acrylic Polymers are as follows:

When a monomer is converted to polymer the conversion may not be complete and the polymeric material may contain some residual monomer. The amount of unpolymerized material strongly depends on the conditions during polymerization. Therefore acrylic bone cements most certainly result in at least some contamination of the biological system with monomeric material. The effects of monomers on cardiovascular system include a transient drop of blood pressure, cardiovascular and pulmonary complications and embolism.

Another aspect of the biocompatibility of acrylic resins is due to the fact that they are capable of causing allergic reactions. Some individuals who received acrylic dentures have complaints of sore mouth and a burning sensation accompanied by symptoms such as swollen oral mucosa.

## VI. Poly Methyl Methacrylate (PMMA):

It is a hard brittle polymer that appears to be unsuitable for most clinical applications, but it does have several important characteristics. It can be prepared under ambient conditions so that it can be manipulated in the operating theater or dental clinic, explaining its use in dentures and bone cement. The relative success of many joint prosthesis is dependent on the performance of the PMMA cement, which is prepared intra operatively by mixing powdered polymer with monomeric methylmethacrylate, which forms a dough that can be placed in the bone, where it then sets. It chemical structure is as follows:

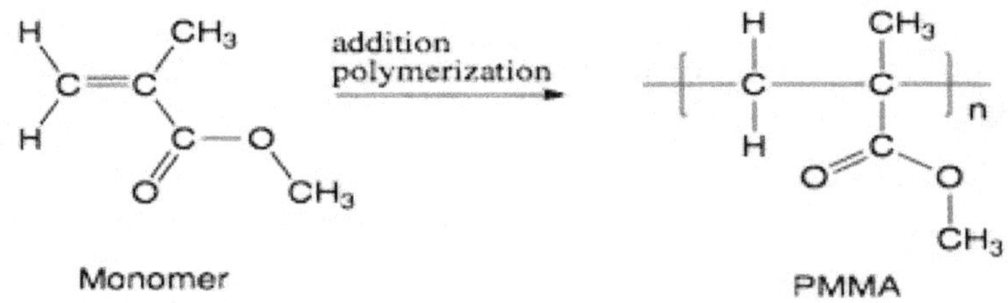

PMMA is a transparent thermoplastic, often used as a light weight or shatter resistant alternative to glass. PMMA is an economical alternative to polycarbonate when extreme strength is not necessary. PMMA does not contain the potentially harmful bisphenol-A subunits found in polycarbonate. It is often preferred because of its moderate properties, easy handling processing and low cost. PMMA can achieve high scratch and impact resistance. PMMA is a strong and light-weight material. It has a density of 1.17-1.20 g/cm^3 which is less than half that of glass.

It has also good impact strength, higher than both glass and polystyrene. Commercial PMMA is an amorphous material with good resistance to dilute alkaline and other inorganic solutions.

PMMA is best known for its exceptional light transparency (92% transmission), high refractive index (1.49) and good weathering properties and as one of the most biocompatible polymers. PMMA can be easily machined with conventional tools, molded, surface coated and plasma etched with glow or corona discharge. PMMA is used in a bone cement. Bone cement has been used for clinical applications to secure a firm fixation of joint prosthesis for hip and knee joints. In orthopedic surgery, PMMA bone cement is used to affix implants and to remodel of lost bone.

In dentures are often made of PMMA, and can be color-matched to the patient's teeth and gum tissue. PMMA is used broadly in medical application such as a blood pump and reservoir, an IV system, membranes for blood dialyzer and in vitro diagnostics.

It is also found in contact lenses and implantable ocular lenses due to excellent optical properties, dentures and maxillofacial prosthesis due to good physical and coloring properties and bone cement for joint prosthesis fixation.

## VII. Silicone Rubber:

Silicone rubbers are polymers having the alternate atoms of silicon and oxygen in the main chain with organic side groups attached to the silicon atoms. For medical applications, the most widely used polymer is polydimethyl-siloxane.

Medium and hard grades are made from dimethyl-siloxane copolymerized with a small amount of methylvinyl-siloxane. Softer grades are made from a copolymer of dimethylchlorosilane and methylvinyl-siloxane containing a small amount of phenyl-methyl-siloxane, the latter contributing to softness.

The filler used is a very pure finely divided silica (SiO2) with a particle size of about 30 μm. The amount of filler is usually in the range of 15 to 20% by volume. By careful compounding, one can greatly enhance the mechanical properties.

Low-molecular-weight polymers have low viscosity and can be crosslinked to make a rubberlike material. Silicone rubbers intended for medical purposes must not contain any of wide variety of additives used in organic rubber compounding.

The physical properties of silicone rubbers depend upon the composition and conditions of the curing procedures. By suitable compounding, a wide range in mechanical properties can be achieved with tensile strength ranging from 25 to 100 MN/m2 and extendibility from 100 to 700%. However, one of the major limitations of silicone rubber is poor resistance to tearing. The physical properties of silicone rubber are given in Table.

| Property | Butyl rubber | Natural rubber | Silicone rubbers | |
|---|---|---|---|---|
| | | | Soft (MDX 4-4515) | Hard (MDX 4-4516) |
| Density (g/cm$^3$) | 0.92 | 0.92 | 1.12 | 1.23 |
| Tensile strength (Mpa) | 7-20 | 7-30 | 6 | 7 |
| Elongation (%) | 100-700 | 100-700 | 600 | 350 |
| Elastic modulus | | | varied upto 10 MPa | |

Table 4: Physical properties of types of rubber

Because of its superior blood compatibility over many other materials silicone rubber has been extensively used for cardiovascular applications. Catheters made from silicone rubber are preferred for long-term parenteral nutrition. Catheters made from other materials such as polyethylene; polyvinyl chloride and Teflon have been found to be too stiff or irritating to the tissues.

The replacement of destroyed or diseased finger joints with silicone prostheses is carried routinely. Other applications of silicone rubber are the replacement of carpal bones, toe prostheses and capping temporomandibular joints. Breast augmentation with silicone rubber mammary prothesis is carried out routinely. Silicone rubber has been extensively used in maxillofacial surgery.

Such uses include nasal supports, jaw augmentation, orbital floor repair, and chin augmentation. These can either be carved from a block of silicone rubber or provided as prefabricated prostheses. Other applications of silicone rubber such as artificial bladder, sphincters and testicles are being investigated. Urethral catheters made from silicone rubber are preferred over many other materials since they are less irritating, easier to use and result in a lower incidence of mucus plug formation and crystal deposition.

There have been numerous reports suggesting that the gradual deterioration of the rubber can occur leading to serious failure of prostheses such as artificial heart valves and finger joints. It has been suggested that failure of implants may be due to uptake of lipids from the blood.

## *VIII. Prosthodontic Polymers:*

A wide range of polymers are commonly used for various applications in prosthodontics. **Polymethylmethacrylate (PMMA)** is commonly used for prosthetic dental applications, including the fabrication of artificial teeth, denture bases, dentures, orthodontic wires, temporary or provisional crowns, and for the repair of dental prostheses.

Additional dental applications of PMMA include occlusal splints, printed or milled casts, dies for treatment planning, and the embedding of tooth specimens for research purposes. The unique properties of PMMA, such as its low density, aesthetics, cost-effectiveness, ease of manipulation, and tailorable physical and mechanical properties, make it a suitable and popular biomaterial for these dental applications.

To further improve the properties (thermal properties, water absorption, solubility, impact strength, flexural strength) of PMMA, several chemical modifications and mechanical reinforcement techniques using various types of fibers, nanoparticles, and nanotubes have been reported recently.

Prosthodontic restorations need to be performed in complex oral environments (biofunctionality) without exerting any adverse effects on the surrounding tissues. Therefore, the PMMA used for denture base materials should be biocompatible and should not cause any irritation, toxicity, or mutagenicity to the oral tissues. It should be non-reactive to nutrients, however should chemically bond to artificial teeth.

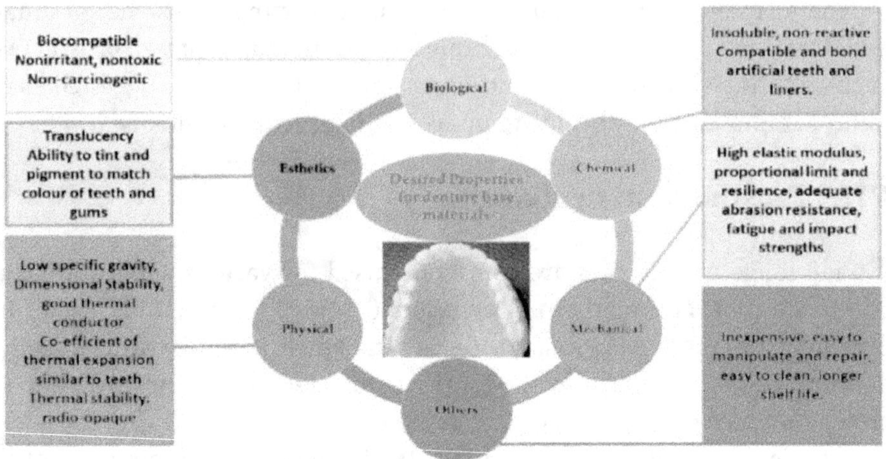


Figure 4: Prosthodontic polymer

Additionally, the PMMA should have good mechanical properties (such as high elastic modulus, proportional limit, resilience, fatigue strength, and impact strength) to withstand the forces of mastication without failure. In addition, other properties such as having low specific gravity (light weight), thermal conductivity, ease of cleaning, and low cost are favorable for patient comfort.

Polymeric acrylic materials are widely used for a range of applications in multiple fields, including engineering, healthcare, and dentistry (Figure 4). In addition to denture bases, other oral healthcare applications for PMMA include fabrication of artificial teeth, impression trays, temporary crowns, obturators for cleft palates, occlusal splints, printed or milled casts, dies for treatment planning, denture relining, and repair.

# IV

# Inflammation and Infection

## Inflammation

It is defined as "local response of living tissues to injury due to any agent.

### *Causes of Inflammation:*

1. **Infective Agents:** Like bacteria, viruses, toxins & fungi
2. **Immunological Agents:** Like cell-mediated and antigen-antibody reactions
3. **Physical Agents:** Like heat, cold, radiation, mechanical trauma
4. **Chemical Agents:** Like organic & inorganic poisons
5. **Inert Materials:** Like foreign bodies

### *Signs of Inflammation:*

1. **Redness (Rubor):** An acutely inflammed tissue appears red due to dilation of small blood vessels within the damaged area (Hyperthermia).

2. **Tumor (Swelling):** Swelling results from edema, the accumulation of fluid in the extravascular space such as part of inflammatory fluid.
3. **Heat (Calor):** Increase in temperature is readily detected in the skin. It is due to increased blood flow (Hyperthermia) through the region, resulting in vascular dilation & the delivery of warm blood to the area.
4. **Pain (Dolor):** Pain results from the stretching & distortion of tissues due to inflammatory edema.
5. **Loss of function:** Examples of a loss of function include not being able to move an inflamed joint properly, having a worse sense of smell during a cold, or finding it more difficult to breathe when you have bronchitis.

Inflammations don't always cause all five symptoms. Some inflammations occur "silently" and don't cause any symptoms.

## *Inflammatory Response:*

1. **Leucocytosis:** White blood cell count increased above the normal range. It is not a disorder or a disease, but a sign of illness.
2. **Endotoxemia:** Bacteria enter the blood stream & release endotoxin. WBC react to the presence of bacteria & release inflammatory substance.
3. **Fever:** Fever is a common systematic response to inflammation.

## Types of Inflammation

There are two types of inflammation, acute and chronic. Acute and chronic inflammation have different causes, symptoms, and purposes.

**Acute Inflammation:** Acute inflammation is typically caused by injuries, like a sprained ankle, or by illnesses, like bacterial infections and common viruses. The acute inflammation process happens quickly and can be severe. If you've ever broken a bone or cut yourself, you've seen inflammation in action. Common signs of inflammation following an injury include:

- Redness
- Pain and tenderness
- Swelling, bumps, or puffiness
- Warmth at the injury site

- Bruising
- Stiffness & Loss of mobility

Depending on the cause and severity of the wound, acute inflammation can last anywhere from a few days to a few months. Sometimes acute inflammation is localized to one area and sometimes it is systemic, as with a viral infection. When your body identifies a harmful invader, such as a bacteria or virus, it initiates a whole-body immune response to fight it off.

White blood cells trigger the release of several inflammatory chemicals. This type of acute inflammation causes you to feel sick and exhausted, as your body puts all of its energy toward fighting off infection.

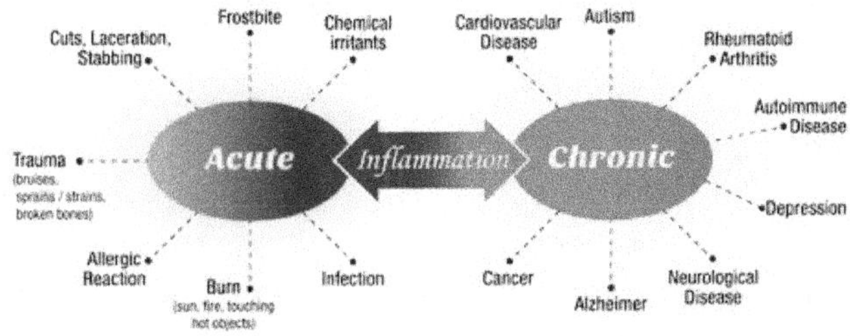


Figure 1: Types of Inflammation

Signs and symptoms may be present for a few days or weeks, or possibly longer in more serious causes.Symptoms of this type of inflammation include:

1. Fever
2. Nausea
3. Lethargy
4. Sleepiness
5. Irritability
6. Runny nose
7. Sore throat
8. Stuffy nose
9. Headache

**Chronic Inflammation:** Chronic, long-term inflammation can last for years or even an entire lifetime. It often begins when there is no injury or illness present, and it lasts far longer than it should. Chronic inflammation is one of several contributing factors in disease onset and progression. So far, the strongest link between chronic inflammation and disease has been seen in type 2 diabetes and heart disease. Other conditions associated with chronic inflammation include:

1. High blood pressure
2. High cholesterol
3. Kidney disease
4. Various types of cancer
5. Depression
6. Neurodegenerative disorders (like Alzheimer's disease)
7. Autoimmune disorders
8. Osteoporosis
9. Fatty liver disease
10. Cancer

Chronic inflammation often progresses quietly, with few independent symptoms. Despite its subtlety, chronic inflammation represents a major threat to the health and longevity of a large population of individuals.

## Difference between Acute & Chronic Inflammation

| Features | Acute | Chronic |
|---|---|---|
| Onset | Rapid | Delayed |
| Duration | Few days | Upto months, years |
| Specificity | Non-specific | Specific (Involves acquired immunity) |
| Signs | Pain, Heat, Redness, Swelling & Loss of Function | Absent |
| Fundamental Cells | Neutrophils, Mast cells, Platelets, Basophil | Macrophages, Plasma cells, Antibodies |
| Causative Agents | Bacteria, Injured tissues | Persistent acute, foreign body, Viral auto immune |

Table 1: Difference between Acute and Chronic Inflammation

# Infection

An infection occurs when another organism enters your body & causes disease. The organisms that cause infections are very diverse & can include things like viruses, bacteria, fungi & parasites. Human can acquire an infection in many different ways, such as directly from a person with an infection, via contaminated food or water, and even though the bite of an insect.

**Types of Infection:**

**Viral Infections:** Virus are very tiny infectious organisms. They are even smaller than bacteria. Virus is composed of a piece of genetic material that is surrounded by a protein shell.

Examples:

1. Flu (influeza)
2. Common cold
3. Chicken pox
4. Polio
5. Norovirus
6. HIV

7. Hepatitis C

**Possible treatments:** Antiviral drugs

**Bacterial Infections:** Bacteria are single cells microorganisms. They are very diverse coming in a variety of different shapes & sizes. It can be found in environment, including soil, bodies of water, and in our bodies. Some can survive extreme temperatures or even radiation exposure. Some bacteria are present in air bodies & these bacterias don't cause disease. In fact, the bacteria in our digestive tract can help us digest our food. However, sometimes bacteria can enter our bodies & cause an infection.

Examples:

1. Throat Infection
2. Bacterial UTIS (Urinary tract infections) caused by coliform bacteria
3. Bacterial food poisoning caused by E-coli
4. Bacterial vaginosis
5. TB (Tuberculosis)
6. Cholera
7. Pneumonia

**Possible treatments:** Bacterial Infections are most often treated with antibiotics. Antibiotics are medications that affect bacterial growth.

**Fungal Infections:** Fungi are another diverse group of organisms that can include things like yeasts & molds. It can be found throughout the environment, including in the soil, indoors in moist areas like bathrooms and or in our bodies. Sometimes fungi are too small that you can't see them with the naked eye.

Examples:

1. Vaginal yeast infections
2. Athlete's foot
3. Ringworm

**Possible treatments:** Antifungal medications for e.g. Ringworm or athlete's foot can be treated with antifungal cream.

**Parasitic Infections:** Parasites live on or in a host organism & get food or other nutrient's at the host's expense.

**Types:**

1.  Protozoa: small one celled organisms
2.  Helminths: larger, warm like organisms
3.  Ectoparasites: Organisms like such as fleas, ticks & lice.

Examples: Malaria, tapeworm infection, pubic & head lice, scabies (types of skin disease)
**Possible treatments:** Drugs (Antiparasitic Medications)

# V
# Cardiac And Ophthalmic Implants

## Cardiac Implants

### *Stent*

A stent is a device made of inert (pure) material and design to serve as the temporary or permanent internal device to maintain or increase the lumen of the vessel. In recent years this device is widely used because of the increased frequency of restenosis following the angioplasty. Main four design are available:

**Spring like design** which is initially having small diameter and it expends to a predetermined dimension when a constraint is removed.

**Balloon expandable stents** which operate on principle of deformation of metals.

**Thermal memory stent** in which the memory metal NITINOL is used and changes its shape depending upon the body temperature.

**Stent made up of biodegradable polymers** which serves as device to increase and maintain the lumen diameter and in addition it may serve as drug delivery device as the drug containing polymers are degradable.

Some of the essential features of stent are:

1. Biocompatibility
2. Reliable
3. Flexibility
4. Expandability
5. Visible by X-rays

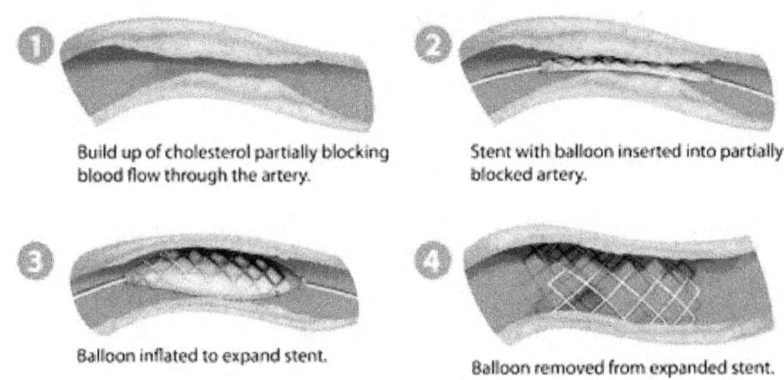



Figure 1: Types of stent

The main possible problems with the stent include:

1. Injury to the vessel wall which is caused by during the insertion of the stent.
2. Formation of the thrombus.

But the incidence of failure caused by thrombosis and restenosis is lower with the stent than with the angioplasty.

**Materials:**

- Stainless steel
- Nitinol
- Polymer

Stent diameter is usually 0.8 to 2.00 mm and length is 15-30 mm.

## Cardiac Assisting Devices

A circulatory Assist Device, also known as a Ventricular assist device is a mechanical circulatory machine. The pumps are used on a short term basis to allow the patient's heart to rest while it is healing. However, they have also been used on a long-term basis to support the heart of patients awaiting a heart transplant. There are three major types of devices:

1. **Intra-aortic Balloon Pump (IABP)**
2. **Left Ventricular Assist Device (LVAD)**


## Intra-aortic Balloon Pump (IABP):

The Intra-aortic balloon pump (IABP) is a mechanical device that is used to decrease myocardial oxygen demand while at the same time it increasing cardiac output. By increasing cardiac output it also increases coronary blood flow and therefore myocardial oxygen delivery. It consists of a cylindrical balloon that sits in the aorta. That is, it actively deflates in systole increasing forward blood flow by reducing afterload, and actively inflates in diastole increasing blood flow to the coronary arteries.

An intra-aortic balloon pump (IABP) is a type of therapeutic device. It helps the heart pump more blood. It may be needed if heart is unable to pump enough blood to body. The IABP consists of a thin, flexible tube called a catheter. Attached to the tip of the catheter is a long balloon. This is called an intra-aortic balloon, or IAB. The other end of the catheter attaches to a computer console. This console has a mechanism for inflating and deflating the balloon at the proper time when heart beats.

Heart pumps oxygenated blood and nutrients to all parts of the body. Blood leaves the heart through the arteries, the blood vessels that carry oxygenated blood. The outer walls of the heart also contain arteries. These are called the coronary arteries. Through these vessels, the heart receives the oxygen and nutrients it needs.

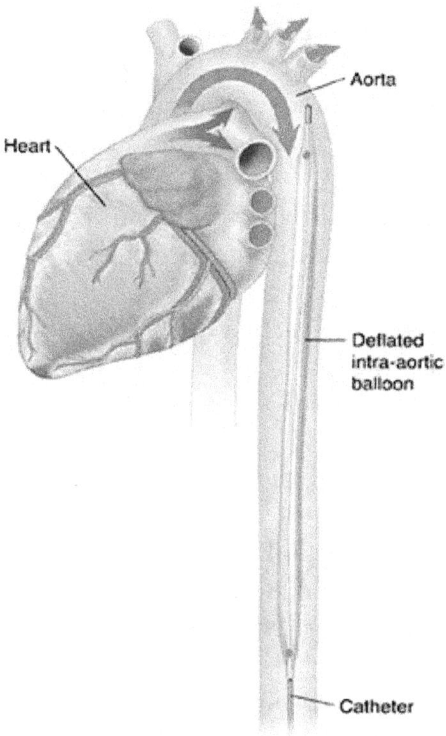


Figure 2: Intra-aortic Balloon Pump (IABP)

When the heart contracts, it sends blood out to the body. As it relaxes, blood flows into the coronary arteries to bring oxygen to the heart. An IABP allows blood to flow more easily into your coronary arteries. It also helps the heart pump more blood with each contraction. The balloon is inserted into the aorta. The aorta is the very large artery leaving the heart. In many cases, this procedure is done through a small cut on the inside of your upper leg.

From there, the IABP can start to do its work. The balloon is set to inflate when the heart relaxes. It pushes blood flow back toward the coronary arteries. They may not have been receiving enough blood without the pump. When the heart contracts, the balloon deflates. That allows the heart to pump more blood out to the body while using less energy. The device continues to inflate and deflate until it is removed.

The device deflates when the heart pumps, so blood can flow to the rest of your body. It inflates when the heart relaxes to keep more blood in the heart.

IABP allows blood to flow more easily into the coronary arteries (arteries in the outer walls of the heart). IABP also helps the heart pump more blood with each contraction. IABP is a short-term treatment. It is usually needed till the heart condition improves or till a permanent treatment is performed. It can be performed after the following heart problems:

- Arrhythmia (irregular heartbeat or rhythm)
- Myocarditis (infection of the heart muscle)
- Heart attack
- An IABP may be used to help recover from surgery to reopen or bypass a blocked artery near the heart.

## *Left Ventricular Assist Device (LVAD):*

A left ventricular assist device (LVAD) is implanted in the chest. It helps pump blood from the lower left heart chamber (left ventricle) to the rest of the body. A control unit and battery pack are worn outside the body and are connected to the LVAD through a small opening (port) in the skin.

It has three parts: an electrically driven mechanical pump, an electronic controller and a power supply. The pump is about 1.5 pounds, made of titanium with a biological friendly lining. It is placed in the abdominal cavity, the LVAD takes blood from the left ventricle and pumps it into the aorta. The LVAD normally pumps at a rate of 60-80 beats per minute, but can increase to 120 beats/minute with exercise.

Two external batteries, via a cable through the abdomen, supply the power for this pump. They are carried in underarm holsters or a waist pack. The electrical controller is a small computer like components that adjust functions of the pump, such as pumping speed.

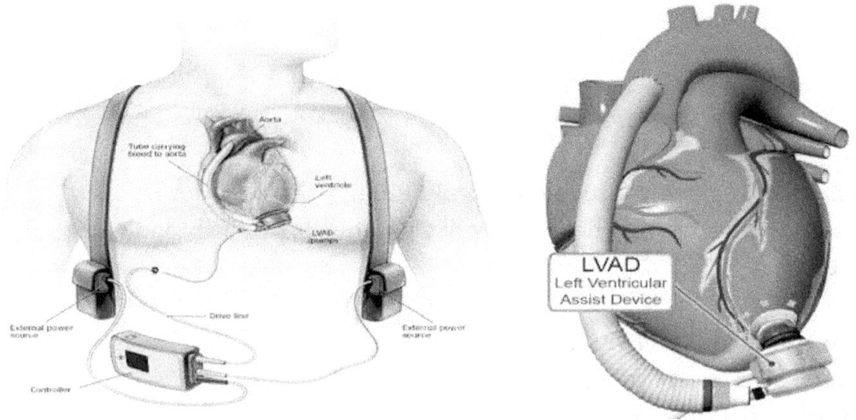


Figure 3: Left Ventricular Assist Device

A tube passes from the device through the skin. This tube, called the driveline connects the pump to the external controller and power source. The pump and its connections are implanted during open heart surgery. A computer controller, a power pack and a reserve power pack remains outside the body. Some models let a person wear these external units on a belt or harness-outside. The power pack has to be recharged at night.

**Benefits of LVAD:**

An LVAD restores blood flow to a person whose heart has been weakened by heart disease. This helps relieve some symptoms such as being constantly tired or short of breath. And sometimes it lets the heart recover normal function by giving it to a chance to rest.

It maintains or improves other organ functions, improves exercise performance, and enables participation in cardiac rehabilitation.

LVADs are now portable and are often used for weeks to months. Patients with LVADs can be discharged from the hospital and have an acceptable quality of life while waiting for a donor heart to become available.

**Risks of LVAD:**

- Infection
- Internal bleeding
- Heart failure
- Device failure

- Blood clots
- Stroke

## *Heart Valve Prosthesis*

Attempts of replacing diseased natural human valves with prosthesis began about four decades ago. The heart valve prosthesis can be broadly classified into three types:

1. **Mechanical Heart Valve**
2. **Biological Heart Valve**
3. **Synthetic Heart Valve**

## *I. Mechanical Heart Valve:*

There are basically three types of Mechanical heart valves:

- **Caged ball valve**
- **Tilting disc valve**
- **Bileaflet valve**

**Caged ball valve:**

The caged ball design is one of the early mechanical heart valve, in that a small ball is held in place by a welded metal cage.

**Material:** Ball is made up of Polymers like Polypropylene or Metals like Titanium and Co-Cr alloy.

The ball in cage design was modelled after ball valve used in industry to limit the flow of fluid to a single direction. Natural valves allow blood to flow straight to the centre of the valve, this property is known as central flow, which keeps the amount of work done by the heart to minimum. With the non-central flow the heart must work harder to compensate for the momentum cost due to the change in direction of fluid. Caged ball valve completely block central flow, so the blood require more energy to flow around the central ball and the ball is notorious for causing damage to blood cells due to collision. Damaged blood cells release clotting substances so that the patient requires life-long anti-coagulant.

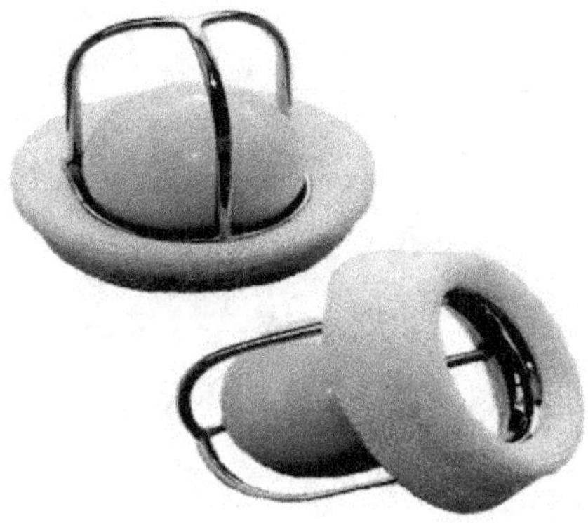

Figure 4: Caged ball valve

**Tilting disc valve:**

For a decade and a half the caged ball valve remained the best design. In the mid 1960 a new class of prosthetic valves were designed that used a tilting disc to better mimic (copy) the natural pattern of blood flow.

**Material:** Disc is made up of Pyrolytic carbon and struts are made up of Co-Cr alloy.

The tilting disc valves have a polymer disc held in place by two welded struts. The disc floats between two struts in such a way that it closes when the blood begins to travel in backward direction and re-opens when the blood begins to travel in forward direction. The tilting disc valves open at an angle of 60 degree and close completely at a rate of 70 times per minute. This valve pattern provide improved central flow while still preventing the backflow of blood. These valves reduce mechanical damage to blood cells and the improved flow pattern and reduces the chances of blood clotting & infection.

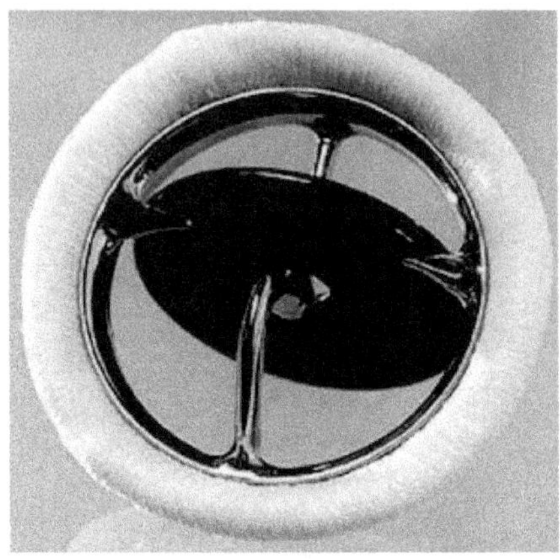

Figure 5: Tilting disc valve

**Disadvantage:** The only problem with this design is its tendency for the outlet struts to fracture as a result of fatigue from the repeated ramming of the struts by the disc. [Ramming: When the blood passes through valve the chances of hit]

**Bileaflet valve:**

In 1979, a new mechanical valve was introduced which consist of two semi-circular leaflets that pivot on hinges.

**Material:** Valve made up of Pyrolytic carbon for designing.

The carbon leaflet exhibits high strength and excellent biocompatibility. This leaflet open completely parallel to the direction of the blood flow but they do not close completely which allow back-flow of blood. For this reason, bileaflet valve is not ideal valve.

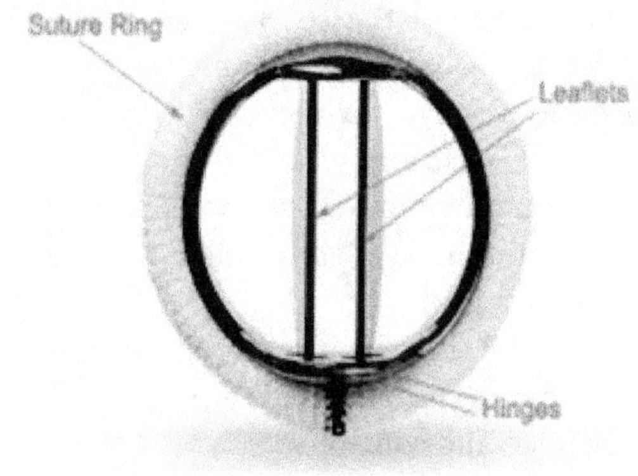


Figure 6: Bileaflet valve

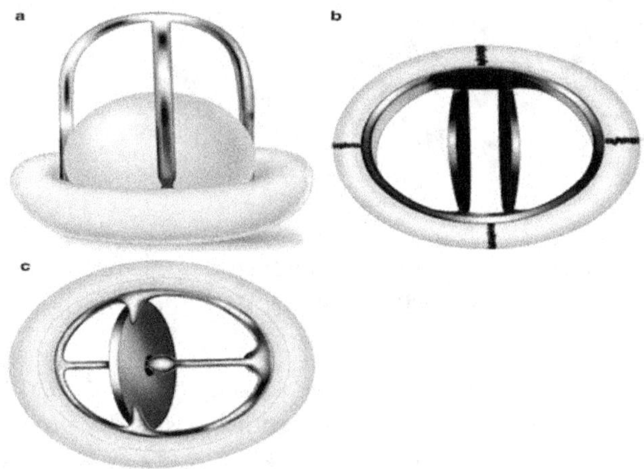


Figure 7: Types of Mechanical Heart Valves

## II.Biological Heart Valve:

The first biological valves implanted were homograft with valves explanted from cadavers within 48 hours after death. Preservation of the valves included various techniques of sterilization, freeze drying and immersing in antibiotic solution. The use of homografts is not popular due to problems with long-term durability & due to limited availability.

Attempts were also made in the early 1960s in the use of xenografts and porcine bio prosthesis became commercially available after the introduction of the gluteraldehyde fixation technique and give the results in improved durability. The valves are harvested from 7- to-12 months old pigs and attached to supporting stents and preserved. The stent provided support to preserve the valve in the natural shape and to achieve normal opening and closing. This is the porcine bio prosthesis.

Fixed bovine pericardial tissue is also used to construct heart valves in which design characteristics such as orifice area, valve height and degree of capitation can be specified and controlled.

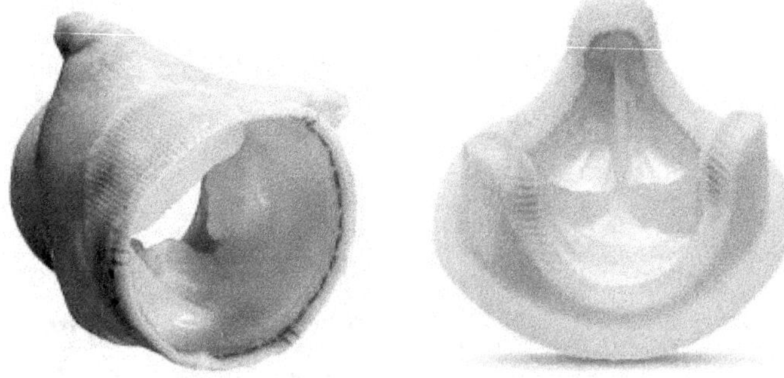

Figure 8: Biological Heart Valves: (a) Porcine [Pig] Heart Valve Prosthesis and (b) Bovine [Cow] Heart Valve Prosthesis

Thus the geometry and flow dynamics past pericardial prosthesis mimic those of the natural human aortic valves more closely. Due to the low profile design of pericardial prosthesis and increased orifice area, these valves are less stenotic compared to porcine bio prosthesis, especially in smaller sizes.

The advantage with bio prosthesis is the freedom from thrombo-embolism and hence not requiring long-term anticoagulant therapy in general. These prosthesis are preferable in patients who do not tolerate anticoagulants. On the other hand, bio prosthetic valves are prone to calcification and leaflet tear with an average life time of about 10 years before replacement is necessary generally attributed to the tissue fixation process.

## III.Synthetic Heart Valve:

Concurrently, efforts have also been made in the development of valve prosthesis made of synthetic material. Several attempts to make bileaflet and trileaflet valves made of polyurethanes, polyester fabrics and silicone rubber were not successful due to problems with durability of relatively thin leaflets made of synthetic material.

Implantation of synthetic trileaflet valves, even more recently has resulted in limited success due to leaflet failure and calcification.

## Implantable Pacemaker

The rhythmic beating of the heart is due to the triggering pulses that originate is an area of specialized tissue in the right atrium of the heart. This area is known as the Sino-atrial node. A pacemaker is a small device that's placed in the chest or abdomen to help control abnormal heart rhythms. This device uses electrical pulses to recover the heartbeat at a normal rate. Pacemakers are used to treat arrhythmia. During an arrhythmia, the heart can beat too fast, too slow, or with an irregular rhythm.

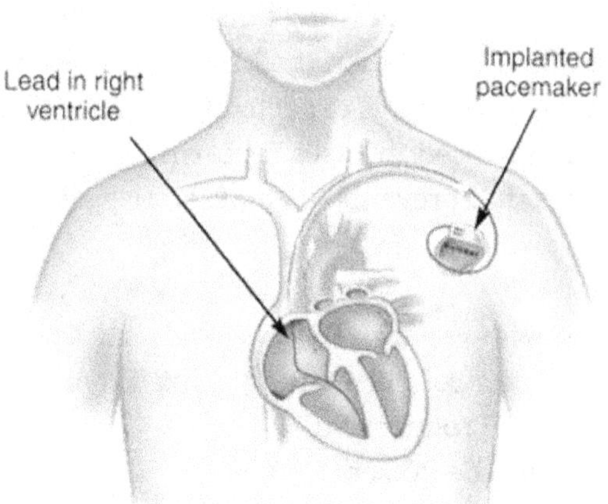


Figure 9: Implantable Cardiac Pacemaker

A heartbeat that's too fast is called tachycardia. A heartbeat that's too slow is called bradycardia. A pacemaker basically consists of two parts:

1. **An electronic unit–** generates stimulating impulses of controlled rate and amplitude, known as pulse generator
2. **The lead–** interface with electrode and terminate within the heart

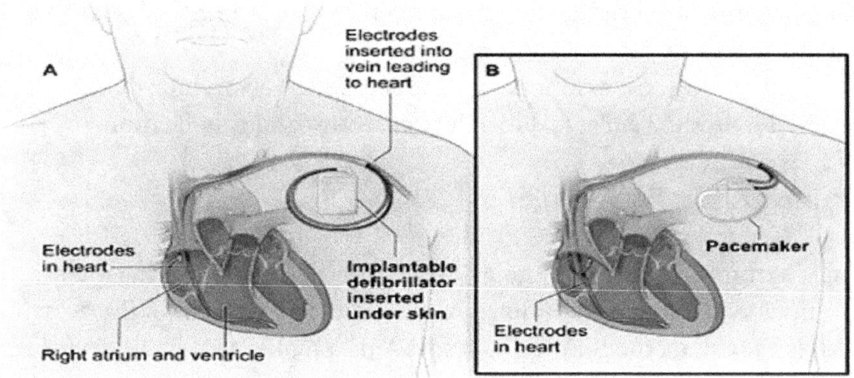


Figure 10: Implantable Pacemaker

The classification of pacemakers into different types is based on the modes of application of the stimulating pulses to the heart.

**External pacemaker–** used when the heart block (SA Node not working) presents as an emergency and it is expected to be present for a short time.

**Internal pacemaker–** used in cases requiring long-term pacing because of permanent damage that prevents normal self triggering of the heart.

Components of Cardiac Pacemakers:

1. Power Supply - provides energy
2. Oscillator Circuit - Control Pulse rate (e.g. fixed rate 70bpm )
3. Pulse output Circuit - Produces Pulse
4. Lead Wires - Conduct the Pulses
5. Electrodes - Transmit Pulses to the tissue
6. Power Supply: Lithium iodide cell which provides a long-term battery life.

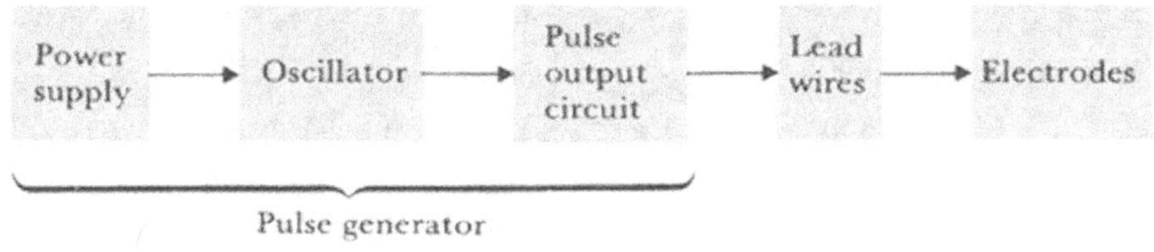


Figure 11: Block-diagram of an asynchronous cardiac pacemaker

## *Grafts*

Grafting refers to a surgical procedure to move tissue from one site to another on the body, or from another creature, without bringing its own blood supply with it. The graft can be classified into four major types.

**Autograft:** The tissue of the original donor is grafted back into the same donor. For example, skin graft from thigh to face in severely deformed case of burnt individuals (plastic surgery).

**Isograft:** Graft between genetically identical individuals (i.e., monozygotic twins)

**Allograft (Homograft):** Graft between allogenic individuals (i.e., members of the same species but of different genetic constitution. For example, kidney transplanted from one human to another.

**Xenograft (Heterograft):** Graft between xenogenic individuals (i.e., different genetic lineage). For example organ transplanted from pig to human, cow to human.

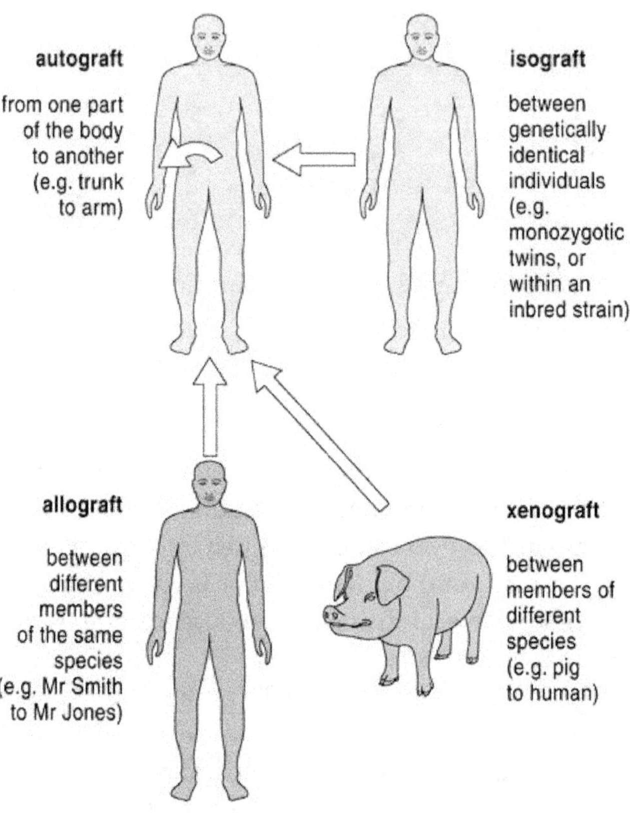


Figure 12: Types of Grafts

## *Vascular Grafts*

Arterial replacement or wall strengthening can be done by opening completely blocked arteries using vein autograft, prosthesis, reinforcement by stent, and with or without embedded stent. Vein implants have more problems than arteries because of the collapse of a nearby vein or clot formation, which in turn causes lower blood pressure than the arteries and stagnant blood flow in the veins. Polymer materials have been used for the formulation of implants, including nylon, polyester, polytetrafluoroethylene, polypropylene, polyacrylonitrile, and silicone rubber.

Primarily responsible for grafting failures within 30 days after implantation is due to thrombosis and internal hyperplasia formation is the cause of failure within 6 months after surgery. Immediately after implantation, layers of fibrin and fibrous bronchial tissue cover the inner and outer surfaces of the prosthesis, respectively. Fibrin replace the layer of fibroblasts is known neointima.

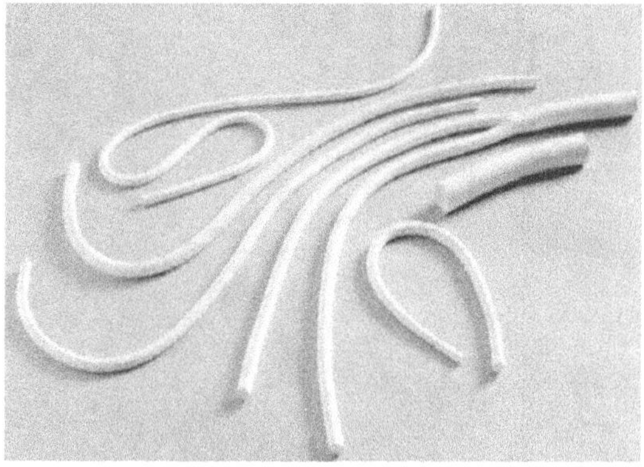

Figure 13: Vascular Grafts

# Ophthalmic Implants

## *Applications of Biomaterials in Ophthalmology*

Ophthalmology is a branch of medicine that has been seen many technological advances in recent years. Lasers are used for imaging and treating many eye conditions and their capabilities are further enhanced by computers and culminate in the integration of devices with neuronal elements to produce "artificial vision". In virtually all endeavours to develop therapies involving eye surgery, biomaterials play a central part.

**Contact lenses** are worn on the corneal surface to improve visual acuity in place of spectacles.

**Corneal Implants, or Keratoprosthesis** have been designed to replace diseased or damaged cornea that have become opaque.

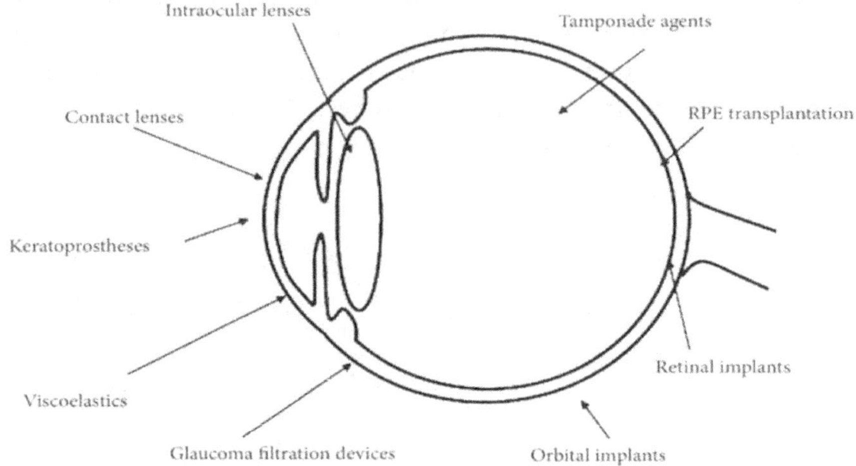


Figure 14: Applications of Biomaterials in Ophthalmology

**Intraocular lenses** are implanted following cataract surgery to replace the opaque crystalline lens.

**Viscoelastic substances** have revolutionized cataract surgery enabling the first truly "Key-hole" operations.

**Glaucoma filtration devices,** are used to produce a channel for the outflow of aqueous to prevent the increase in intra ocular pressure.

**Tamponade agents** are used to replace the vitreous and treat retinal detachment.

**Retinal implants** are designed to transmit electrical signals to the brain via the retina and the optic nerve.

Biomaterials are exploited for their various physical properties to achieve the goals of surgery. There are a number of essential requirements that need to be addressed by ophthalmic biomaterials which include the ability to deliver oxygen to the tissues, modification of refraction, protection of tissues during surgery, integration with the tissues, modulation of wound healing and tamponading of retinal breaks.

In the field of ophthalmology, more flexible biomaterials are used for improve the mechanical integrity of the tissue/implant interface. For example, Silicones and Polyurethane.

**List of Biomaterials used in Ophthalmology:**

- Polymethyl methacrylate (PMMA)
- Hydroxyapatite (HA)
- Porous Polyethylene (PP)
- Bio ceramic
- Poly (2-hydroxyethyl methacrylate) (PHEMA)
- Cellulose acetate butyrate
- Silicone
- Hydrogel
- Polydimethylsiloxane
- Polytetrafluoroethylene (PTFE)

Thus, these all materials are used in the application of ophthalmology like contact lens, Intraocular lens, Keratoprosthesis, Retinal Implants, Viscoelastic, Orbital Implants etc.

## *Contact Lens*

Contact lenses are thin, curved plastic disks designed to cover the cornea, the clear front covering of the eye. Contact lenses are used to correct the same conditions that eyeglasses correct:

- Myopia (nearsightedness)
- Hyperopia (farsightedness)
- Astigmatism (distorted vision)
- Presbyopia (need for bifocals)

**Materials:**

1. Cellulose acetate butyrate
2. PMMA
3. PHEMA
4. Siloxane Methacrylate
5. Silicones

**Required Properties of Contact lenses:**

Contact lenses are optical devices that must have good transition of visible light. Pigments and dyes are added to some contact lens for cosmetic effect. Contact lenses also may have UV light absorbing additives which is usually co-polymerized in the contact lens material. In addition to the required optical properties chemical stability and amiability to be manufactured at reasonable cost, have high oxygen transmissibility.

Contact lens must be easy to clean and disinfect. Most contact lenses wear developed with the important property of oxygen permeability. For oxygen permeability the ideal contact lens would be made of poly-dimethyl siloxane.

For better mechanical property & manufactures most silicone elastomeric lenses have been made of diverse poly-methyl phenyl vinyl siloxane. Silicone rubber lenses have not been very successful for general cosmetic use not only because of surface problems and comfort because they have a strong tendency to adhere to the cornea.

### Types of Contact lenses:

Many types of contact lenses are available. The type of contacts you use depends on your particular situation. Your eye doctor will be able to help you choose from the following types of lenses.

Materials placed in direct contact with the cornea to correct the vision have been used for over 20 years.

### 1.PMMA lenses: (Hard/Non-Permeable/Rigid)

PMMA was the first material used for contact lens because of its superior optical properties. Rigid or hard contact lenses were the first lenses. They are made of a type of plastic called PMMA (Poly-methylmethacrylate), which is very durable, but does not allow oxygen in the air to directly reach the cornea.

When the eye blinks, the lens moves which allows the oxygen dissolved in the tears to reach the cornea. Rigid (Hard) lenses are the least comfortable type of contact lenses and are not really used anymore. Some people still prefer them for their durability and lower cost.

### 2. Gas-Permeable lenses: (Hard)

These lenses are also known as "RGPs". They are newer rigid or "hard" lenses made of plastics combined with other materials, such as silicone and fluoropolymers, which allow oxygen in the air to pass directly through the lens. For this reason, they are called "Gas Permeable".

### 3.Soft Contact lenses:

These lenses are made of plastic materials that incorporate water. The water makes them soft and flexible, as well as allowing oxygen to reach the cornea. More than 75% of contact lenses wearers in the united states use soft lenses.

**Advantages & Disadvantages of Soft and Hard Contact Lenses:**

| Type | Advantages | Disadvantages |
|---|---|---|
| Soft Permeable | - High Oxygen Permeability | - Deposition of Lipomucoprotein & bacterial growth |
| Rigid Non Permeable | - Optical Properties | - Low Oxygen Permeable |
| Rigid Gas Permeable (RGPs) | - High Oxygen Permeability | - Accumulation of surface deposites |

Table 1: Advantages and Disadvantages of Contact Lenses

**Problems associated with lenses:**

1. Hyper sensitive reaction
2. Infection
3. Toxicity
4. Hypoxia

**Disposable contact lenses:**

Disposable Contact Lenses are lenses designed to be replaced on a regular basis usually daily, by-weekly or monthly. The more often a lens is replaced the less likely the lens will become deposited with proteins and oils. Many problems that contact lens wearers experienced in the past when lenses were replaced on an annual or two yearly bases are seldom seen nowadays.

Disposable contact lenses are therefore a healthier alternative. Daily disposable contact lenses are a great option for people who only want to wear their contact lenses a few times a week for example for sport or forgoing out at night.

They also remove the need for cleaning, since they are inserted in the morning(before the start of your day / play sport / work) and then thrown away at the end of the day offering exceptional convenience and good value for money. Lenses, which are replaced on a two-weekly or monthly basis, are good value if you want to wear lenses every day.

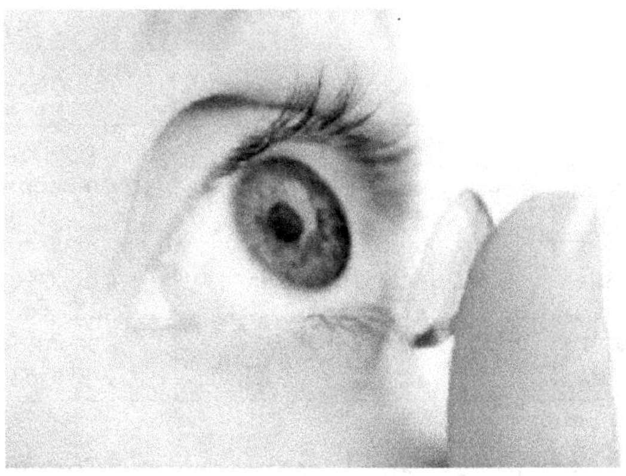

Figure 15: Disposable contact lens

## *Intraocular Lenses (IOLs)*

**Materials used in IOLs:**

1. Polymethyl methacrylate (PMMA)
2. Hydroxyapatite (HA)
3. Porous Polyethylene (PP)
4. Bioceramic
5. Poly (2-hydroxyethyl methacrylate) (PHEMA)

**Polymethyl methacrylate (PMMA):** PMMA is a transparent thermoplastic available for use as ocular prosthesis, replacement of intraocular lenses when the original lens has been removed in the treatment of cataracts and has historically been used as hard contact lenses. PMMA has a good degree of compatibility with human tissue, much more so than glass.

**Hydroxyapatite (HA):** Hydroxyapatite implants are spherical and made in a variety of sizes and different material. The porous nature of this material allows fibro vascular ingrowth throughout the implant and permits insertion of a coupling device with reduced risk of inflammation or infection associated with earlier types of exposed integrated implants. The main disadvantages of HA is that it needs to be covered with exogenous material such as sclera, dacron or vicryl mesh, as direct suturing is not possible for muscle attachment. Scleral covering carries with it the risk of transmission of infection, inflammation and rejection.

**IOL Benefits:** Virtually everyone develops cataracts later in life; they are an inevitable part of growing old. Replacement of the eye's natural crystalline lens is the only treatment proven effective for this vision obscuring problem.

The benefits of intraocular lenses, including improved vision and less reliance on corrective lenses for outweigh IOL risks as advances in intraocular lens technology and surgical implantation techniques have made cataract surgery safe and very effective.

The benefits of IOL extend as well to individuals who have presbyopia, the gradual decline of near vision that begins in middle age as the eye's natural crystalline lens loses flexibility. Multifocal intraocular lenses can alleviate the effects of presbyopia and eliminate or greatly reduce the need for reading glasses.

**IOL Safety:** After years of rigorous testing in Europe, Asia, and in the United states by the Food and Drug Administration, IOL and implantation surgery have been proven safe and effective, with complications occurring in less than 5% of cases. IOL risks increase for patients with certain medical conditions and other health-related issues.

Your ophthalmologist will perform a deep examination of your eyes and will research your medical history to ensure that you are a good candidate for intraocular lenses before proceeding with the treatment.

**IOL Convenience:** One of the greatest benefits of intraocular lenses is reduced dependence on glasses and contact lenses. For some patients, the IOL procedure eliminates the need for corrective lenses entirely.

The troubling haze of cataracts disappears, and daily tasks become easier and more enjoyable. The procedure allows some patients to return to driving a car, particularly at night. For patients who have IOL vision correction for presbyopia, reading glasses for many close range tasks, such as reading a menu or a news paper, are often unnecessary.

## *Viscoelastic solutions*

Solutions of macromolecules in a solvent protect cells from mechanical damage, separate and lubricate tissues, allow manipulation of tissues while limiting mechanical damage. Therefore they are used during insertion of intraocular lenses, removal of cataract and to maintain retinal position.

| Device or procedure | Medical application |
| --- | --- |
| Contact lens | Correct vision |
| Intraocular lens | Replace lens containing cataracts |
| Epikeratoplasty | Change corneal curvature and correct vision |
| Scleral buckling materials | Indent detached retina |
| Viscous polymer solutions | Insertion in intraocular lenses, cataract removal and maintain retinal position |

Table 2: Devices/Biomaterials used in Ophthalmology

The ability of a viscoelastic solution to maintain tissue, i.e. maintain space is directly related to its viscosity when at rest. The higher is viscosity at rest, the greater the tissue manipulation capability. The ability of a solution to shear thin, when stress is applied on it is a desirable property as it pertains to the injection of viscoelastic material through small gauge cannulas, for tissue manipulation.

The viscosity and shear thinning of macromolecular solutions depend on several molecular parameters including molecular weight and shape, the nature of intramolecular interactions and interactions between polymer and solvent molecules.

Thus, the desirable properties of a transparent viscoelastic solution include: ability to coat cellular linings, high zero shear rate viscosity, low surface tension, no elevation of intraocular pressure, rapid clearance from eye, biologically inertness, non-toxicity and easy sterilizability.

Since hyaluronic acid (HA) is the major component of vitreous humor, many viscoelastic have been prepared from high molecular weight HA (> 106 D). Extrapure HA at concentrations of 1-3% in phosphate buffered saline at pH 7.2. is used. Operationally, sodium HA solutions have been shown to coat and protect the corneal endothelium during animal surgery, as well as, to protect the endothelium against cell loss incurred by contact with intraocular lenses.

Hydroxy-propyl-methyl-cellulose (HPMC) viscoelastic solutions contain a range of concentrations from 0.5-5% of polymer in a physiological salt solution (i.e. 0.49% NaCI, 0.075% KCI, 0.048% CaCh, 0.03% MgClb 0.39% sodium acetate and 0.17% sodium citrate at pH 7.2). Results of clinical studies indicate that either solutions containing 2% HPMC or those containing 1 % of high molecular weight HA help to maintain normal shape of the anterior chamber and facilitate anterior caps ulotomy and nuclear expression in extracapsular cataract extraction with posterior chamber lens implantation.

A number of macromolecules besides HA and HPMC have been used as viscoelastics including chondroitin sulphate (CS), collagen, other cellulose derivatives and polyacrylamide. All these molecules except collagen and poly-acrylamide are polysaccharides. Clearly all viscoelastics protect against damage to corneal endothelium better than saline solution.

## *Vitreous Implants*

Injectable synthetic polymers are used with increasing frequency in cases of vitreoretinal surgery. Sodium hyaluronate solutions are useful in some of these cases, but their relatively short retention time in the vitreous cavity is a limiting factor. Alternatively, high viscosity silicone oil, usually, poly (dimethyl siloxane), is injected into the vitreous cavity. This procedure is still controversial due to reported complications such as oil emulsification in the anterior chamber, glaucoma and corneal dystrophy.

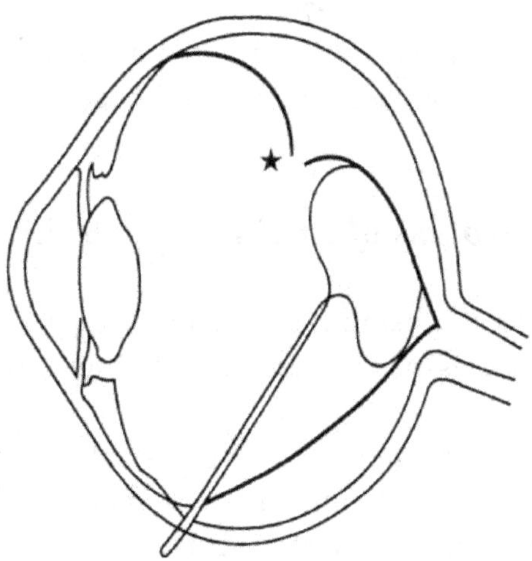

Figure 16: Intravitrial injection of viscous polymer

## Eye shields

These are used in the treatment of basement membrane associated diseases, corneal abrasion and erosion, epithelial defects, cataract extraction, penetrating keratoplasty and other diseases that cause eye inflammation. Once applied to eye these shields absorb fluid from ocular surface and begin to dissolve.

The surface polymers in use are hydrogels, polyvinyl alcohol, silicone rubber and collagen. Thin clear, pliable collagen films (0.0127-0.77 mm thick) in a spherical shell shape with a diameter of -14.5 mm and a base curvature of 9 mm are used as eye shields for relief of discomfort. Since the introduction of the eye shield, ophthalmologists have begun to evaluate its use to prolong the delivery of antibacterial, antifungal, antiinflammatory and antiviral agents.

## Drainage tubes in Glaucoma

Implant materials serve as drainage tubes for a relatively small number of cases of otherwise intractable glaucoma. One end of the tube is placed in the anterior chamber and the other end drains the aqueous fluid into a pocket dissected in the outer walls of the eye.

These tubes have been made of a variety of materials, shapes and forms, but they have not been very successful, mainly due to tendency to plug up by fibrosis.

## Manufacturing process of cardiac/ophthalmic implant

By allowing surgeons to customise implants for patients using selective laser melting, pain and tissue damage, surgery time and recovery time will all be reduced.

The primary disadvantages of current manufacturing procedures for personalised implants are the time and cost required for the design and the possible need for a surgical robot to perform the bone resection. These disadvantages may be eliminated by additive manufacturing technologies, especially the use of selective laser melting to enable quick and economical fabrication of patient specific implant components.

Also, in order to manufacture the personalised implants; the additive manufacturing technology of selective laser melting will be used for reducing the build time for the implants and post-processing will ensure the required quality and accuracy.

The selective laser melting process starts by numerically slicing a 3D CAD model into a number of finite layers. For each sliced layer a laser scan path is calculated which defines both the boundary contour and some form of fill sequence, often a raster pattern.

Each layer is then sequentially recreated by depositing powder layers, one on top of the other, and melting their surface by scanning a laser beam. The powder is spread uniformly by a wiper. A high power-density fibre laser with a 20μm beam spot size fully melts the pre-deposited powder layer. The melted particles fuse and solidify to form a layer of the component.

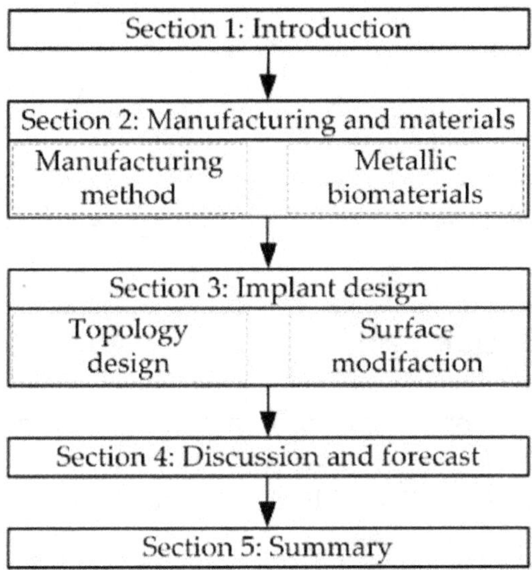


Figure 17: Manufacturing Process of Cardiac & Ophthalmic Implant

# VI
# Orthopedic And Dental Implants

## Orthopedic Implants

### *Temporary fixation devices*

The purpose of temporary fixation devices is to stabilize fractured bone until natural healing processes have restored sufficient strength so that the implant can be removed. These devices include pins, nails, wires, screws, plates, and intramedullary devices.

Bone plates are used for joining bone fragments together during healing of load-bearing bones. The plate provides rigidity for the fixation of the fracture. Screws are used with the plates to secure them to the bone.

There are many different types and sizes of fracture plates describes femoral neck fracture fixation with compression bone plate. Since the forces generated by the muscles in the limbs are very large, femoral and tibial plates must be very strong.

One major drawback of the healing by rigid plate fixation is the weakening of the underlying bone such that refracture may occur following removal of the plate. This is largely due to the stress-shield effect.

Therefore new materials are being evaluated for fabrication of plates with a low axial stiffness and moderate bending and torsional stiffness to facilitate fracture healing without bone atrophy. Another approach is to use a resorb able material for the bone plate. As the strength of the fracture site increases due to natural healing processes, the resorption of the implant begins to take place. The gradual reduction of strength of implant transfers an increasingly larger percent of the load to the healing bone.

The degradation products of such plates must be biocompatible. The design aspect must involve producing the appropriate combination of initial strength and time-dependent performance through the variation in absorption rate and microstructure. There is no need for second operation in removing these plates. However this approach has many limitations and is still in evolutionary stage.

The advantage of an intramedullary device is that it can be nailed through a small incision. When they are inserted, blood supply is interrupted, however vitality of the bone is not damaged. A solid reunion can be achieved with this method of treatment. Removal of nail after a year or two is required for proper healing.

## Fracture healing

The application of electrical energy can enhance osteogenic activity. The tissue can respond to the right amount of energy input (10-40 I1v) without excessive electrical potential (<1 V). The stimulation is also closely related to the nature of electrode material, surface area and location. Noninvasive magnetic stimulators use a pair of Helmholtz coils, which are aligned across the wound site and a magnetic field with a monophasic 150-ms phase with a repetition rate of 75 Hz is applied.

This pulse amplitude induces 1-2 m V fcm of potential in the bone. The efficiency of both magnetic and direct current stimulation is about the same, over 70% success rate. Recent studies indicate that direct electrical stimulation provides a significant improvement in bone ingrowth, while pulsed electromagnetic field and AC capacitivity coupled electrical stimulation do not help ingrowth enough to be noticed.

## Repair of the ligaments

The ligaments and tendons function in coordination with your muscles, joints, and bones in order for your body to make all movements that are needed during your day-to-day life. The ligaments and tendons are each comprised of tissue that contains fibers. These fibers also have a protein that is called collagen, which is beneficial for your ligaments, tendons, bones, muscles and organ tissues.

Ligaments connect your bones to other bones and provide stability to your joints, while tendons connect the bones to your muscles. There are ligaments that are contained throughout your body, including your knees, shoulders, ankles, wrists, back, neck and elbows.

**Knee Ligaments** – there are four different ligaments that are located in your knees. These are the anterior cruciate ligament (ACL), the posterior cruciate ligament (PCL), the lateral collateral ligament (LCL), and the medial collateral ligament (MCL).

**Elbow Ligaments** – you also have three primary ligaments that are located near your elbow. These are the radial collateral ligament, the annular ligament, and the ulnar collateral ligament. These ligaments supply support to your humerus – which is the long bone of your upper arm – along with the radius and ulna – which are the long bones contained in your forearm.

**Ankle Ligaments** – you also have multiple ligaments that are located near your ankle, including the three ligaments that can be found on the outside of your ankle (anterior talofibular, posterior talofibular, and calcaneofibular). The deltoid ligament is located on the inside of your ankle, while the posterior talofibular ligament can be found at the back of your ankle.

**Shoulder Ligaments** – there are also several ligaments in your shoulder. Some of them are responsible for connecting your humerus to your shoulder blade, which is also called the scapula. There are also ligaments that join your collarbone (or clavicle) to the shoulder blade.

**Hand and Wrist Ligaments** – there are a number of ligaments that are contained in your wrist and hand. These include the collateral, and volar ligaments of your hand, along with the dorsal radiocarpal ulnocarpal and radioulnar ligaments that facilitate the use of your wrists

**Back Ligaments** – The ligaments of your spine supply the stability for your movements while placing limitations on how far you can stretch in any direction. The anterior longitudinal, ligamentum flavum, and posterior longitudinal are among the ligaments that reside in your spine.

**Neck Ligaments** – You also have ligaments in your neck, which preserve the placement of your spinal cord. Your neck is mobile, although that raises the potential for an issue to surface within these ligaments.

**Ligament sprain:** If a particular movement causes your ligaments to stretch, it can result in a sprain. But if a similar stretch involves a tendon, then it is considered to be a strain. Twisting or rolling your ankle can cause a sprain, and this is the most common form of this injury. However, there are other areas of the body that can be impacted by this type of issue.

Any event that forces your ligaments beyond the usual limits of movement can create a sprain in your wrist, neck, and back. This is also the case for a major collision or impact with the ground. However, a sprain of your shoulder ligaments will result in a tear. This can also develop if you attempt to cushion a fall with your arm or hand. That scenario can also cause a sprain in your elbow.

**Ligament tear:** Experiencing a more serious ligament tear can be extremely painful. It might also involve bruising and swelling while moving your joint could also be problematic. In many cases, an individual who tears a ligament might hear a popping sound at the moment of the injury occurs. This can often result from a sudden change in direction such as jumping, landing or from an immediate stop.

**Repair of the ligaments:** The specifics of your knee injury will determine the exact form of treatment. In many cases, surgery will not be required, as a combination of rest, ice, elevation, elastic bandages, physical therapy or pain relief will be recommended. However, if you have experienced a complete tear, your physician will likely recommend surgery in order to repair the ligament.

Repair of a torn ligament will often occur as outpatient surgery. However, there are situations in which it will take place in a hospital. This will be discussed when your doctor delivers his or her recommendation, as will any usage of anesthesia. The actual procedure will usually be undertaken with an arthroscope – which is a thin instrument that is temporarily inserted into your joint.

The actual repair of a torn ligament in the knee will involve reattaching the ligament, or reconstruction of the ligament by replacing it with a small segment of a tendon. The process of arthroscopic surgery is similar for the repair of torn ligaments in the wrist, or elbow. It is also true of injuries involving the repair of torn ligaments in the wrist, ankle, or shoulder.

## *Joint Replacements*

Replacement arthroplasty or joint replacement surgery, is a procedure of orthopedic surgery in which an arthritic or dysfunctional joint surface is replaced with an orthopedic prosthesis. Joint replacement is considered as a treatment when severe joint pain or dysfunction is not alleviated by less-invasive therapies. It is a form of arthroplasty, and is often indicated from various joint diseases, including osteoarthritis and rheumatoid arthritis.

Joint replacement surgery is typically recommended for patients with advanced end stage joint disease (usually of the knee or the hip) who have tried non-surgical treatment, but still experience functional decline and disabling pain. Joint replacement is an extremely effective surgery when done at the right time and indication.

Modern joint replacement surgery involves removal of the worn cartilage from both sides of the joint, followed by resurfacing of the joint with a metal and plastic replacement implant that looks and functions much like your normal joint. Although nearly every joint in the body can be replaced, most replacement surgeries involve the hip or knee.

Over the last 30 years, improved surgical techniques and new implant materials have been developed, making total joint replacement one of the most reliable and durable procedures in any area of medicine. Severe or "end-stage" arthritis can be caused by a variety of problems including osteoarthritis, rheumatoid arthritis and other inflammatory joint problems, previous joint injuries and fractures, joint infections and other rare conditions such as osteonecrosis. All of these problems result in damage to the different structures in the joint and eventually lead to significant irreversible damage and dysfunctional joint.

Certain types of arthritis, such as rheumatoid arthritis and other inflammatory types of arthritis may be best treated by a rheumatologist, who specializes in treatment of these disorders. More common joint problems like osteoarthritis are typically treated by a primary care doctor, rheumatologist, or orthopedic surgeon. When medical treatment for arthritis recommended by your doctor becomes less effective, joint replacement surgery may be an option.

## *Total Hip Replacement*

Total hip arthroplasty (THA) is one of the most cost-effective and consistently successful surgeries performed in orthopaedics. THA provides reliable outcomes for patients' suffering from end-stage degenerative hip osteoarthritis (OA), specifically pain relief, functional restoration, and overall improved quality of life. Once considered a procedure limited to the elderly, low-demand patients, THA is becoming an increasingly popular procedure performed in younger patient populations.

During a hip replacement, the head of the femur is replaced with a prosthetic head on a shaft, and the joint surface of the acetabulum is lined with a bowl-shaped synthetic joint surface. A partial hip replacement can also be done for neck of femur fractures where only the femoral part is replaced.

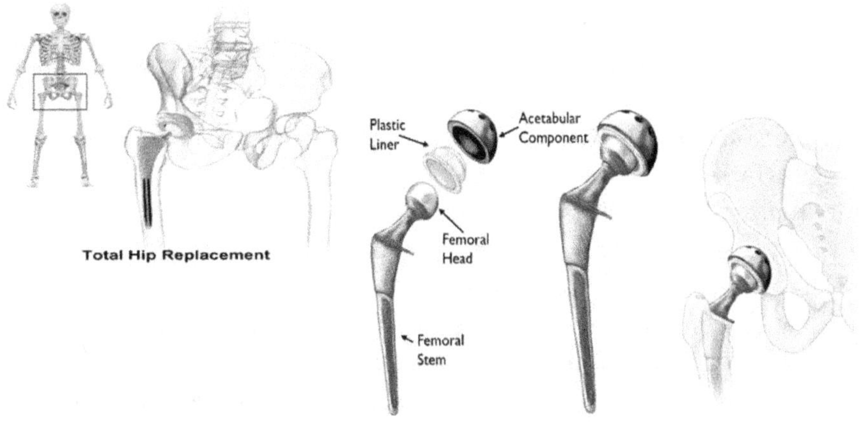


Figure 1: Total Hip Replacement

The hip is a ball and socket joint. This design allows the poly-axial movement seen at the hip.

1. The ball is the femoral head. The head of the femur is gripped by the acetabulum beyond its maximum diameter.
2. The acetabulum (part of the pelvis) is the socket. The acetabulum is cup-shaped, providing the articular surface for the head of the femur to move within.

The head of the femur and the inside of the acetabulum are covered with a layer of hyaline cartilage. Once this cartilage is worn away or damaged (usually by arthritis), the underlying bone is exposed, resulting in pain, stiffness and possibly shortening of the affected leg. By replacing these surfaces the aim is to reduce pain and stiffness to restore an active and pain-free life.

THA prosthetic designs have been evolving since their inception. Contemporary THA techniques have evolved into press-fit femoral and acetabular components.

Bearing surfaces are the surfaces which articulate in the prosthetic joint. The femoral head and the acetabular liner can be used in different combinations. These will give different appearance on radiograph depending on the configuration. Options for bearing surfaces include:

**Metal-on-polyethylene (MoP):** MoP has the longest track record of all bearing surfaces at the lowest cost

**Ceramic-on-polyethylene (CoP):** becoming an increasingly popular option

**Ceramic-on-ceramic (CoC):** CoC has the best wear properties of all THA bearing surfaces

**Metal-on-metal (MoM):** Although falling out of favor, MoM has historically demonstrated better wear properties from its MoP counterpart. MoM has lower linear-wear rates and decreased volume of particles generated. However, the potential for pseudotumor development as well as metallosis-based reactions has resulted in a decline in the use of MoM. MoM is also contraindicated in pregnant women, patients with renal disease, and patients at risk of metal hypersensitivity.

**Femoral Components or Stem:** This refers to the prosthesis which is implanted into the femur. They can be described by length, taper, and presence of a collar. Attached to the femoral component is the neck and head which in most prostheses can be altered in size to create a stable joint.

**Prosthesis Fixation:** Femoral stem fixation can be either cemented or non-cemented (biological) fixation. There is a tendency to use non-cemented femoral stems in younger patients, due to higher reported rates of loosening of cemented stems in long term follow-up. Most common fixation for the acetabular component is non-cemented. Biologic fixation uses either porous coated metallic surface to stimulate bone in growth or grit-blasted surface to allow bone on growth. The prosthesis can also be coated in hydroxyapatite, which is an osteoconductive agent.

During hip replacement, a surgeon removes the damaged sections of the hip joint and replaces them with parts usually constructed of metal, ceramic and very hard plastic. This artificial joint (prosthesis) helps reduce pain and improve function.

Also called total hip arthroplasty, hip replacement surgery might be an option if hip pain interferes with daily activities and nonsurgical treatments haven't helped or are no longer effective. Arthritis damage is the most common reason to need hip replacement. Conditions that can damage the hip joint, sometimes making hip replacement surgery necessary, include:

**Osteoarthritis:** Commonly known as wear-and-tear arthritis, osteoarthritis damages the slick cartilage that covers the ends of bones and helps joints move smoothly.

**Rheumatoid arthritis:** Caused by an overactive immune system, rheumatoid arthritis produces a type of inflammation that can erode cartilage and occasionally underlying bone, resulting in damaged and deformed joints.

**Osteonecrosis:** If there isn't enough blood supplied to the ball portion of the hip joint, such as might result from a dislocation or fracture, the bone might collapse and deform.

Hip replacement may be an option if hip pain:

- Persists, despite pain medication
- Worsens with walking, even with a cane or walker
- Interferes with sleep
- Affects the ability to walk up or down stairs
- Makes it difficult to rise from a seated position

Risks associated with hip replacement surgery can include:

**Blood clots:** Clots can form in the leg veins after surgery. This can be dangerous because a piece of a clot can break off and travel to the lung, heart or, rarely, the brain. Blood-thinning medications can reduce this risk.

**Infection:** Infections can occur at the site of the incision and in the deeper tissue near the new hip. Most infections are treated with antibiotics, but a major infection near the new hip might require surgery to remove and replace the artificial parts.

**Fracture:** During surgery, healthy portions of the hip joint might fracture. Sometimes the fractures are small enough to heal on their own, but larger fractures might need to be stabilized with wires, screws, and possibly a metal plate or bone grafts.

**Dislocation:** Certain positions can cause the ball of the new joint to come out of the socket, particularly in the first few months after surgery. If the hip dislocates, a brace can help keep the hip in the correct position. If the hip keeps dislocating, surgery may be needed to stabilize it.

**Change in leg length:** Surgeons take steps to avoid the problem, but occasionally a new hip makes one leg longer or shorter than the other. Sometimes this is caused by a contracture of muscles around the hip. In these cases, progressively strengthening and stretching those muscles might help. Small differences in leg length usually aren't noticeable after a few months.

**Loosening:** Although this complication is rare with newer implants, the new joint might not become solidly fixed to the bone or might loosen over time, causing pain in the hip. Surgery might be needed to fix the problem.

**Nerve damage:** Rarely, nerves in the area where the implant is placed can be injured. Nerve damage can cause numbness, weakness and pain.

## *Total Knee Replacement*

If your knee is severely damaged by arthritis or injury, it may be hard for you to perform simple activities, such as walking or climbing stairs. You may even begin to feel pain while you are sitting or lying down.

If nonsurgical treatments like medications and using walking supports are no longer helpful, you may want to consider total knee replacement surgery. Joint replacement surgery is a safe and effective procedure to relieve pain, correct leg deformity, and help you resume normal activities.

Knee replacement surgery — also known as knee arthroplasty (ARTH-row-plas-tee) — can help relieve pain and restore function in severely diseased knee joints. The procedure involves cutting away damaged bone and cartilage from your thighbone, shinbone and kneecap and replacing it with an artificial joint (prosthesis) made of metal alloys, high-grade plastics and polymers. In determining whether a knee replacement is right for you, an orthopedic surgeon assesses your knee's range of motion, stability and strength. X-rays help determine the extent of damage. Your doctor can choose from a variety of knee replacement prostheses and surgical techniques, considering your age, weight, activity level, knee size and shape, and overall health.

**Causes:** The most common cause of chronic knee pain and disability is arthritis. Although there are many types of arthritis, most knee pain is caused by just three types: osteoarthritis, rheumatoid arthritis, and post-traumatic arthritis.

**Osteoarthritis:** This is an age-related "wear and tear" type of arthritis. It usually occurs in people 50 years of age and older, but may occur in younger people, too. The cartilage that cushions the bones of the knee softens and wears away. The bones then rub against one another, causing knee pain and stiffness.

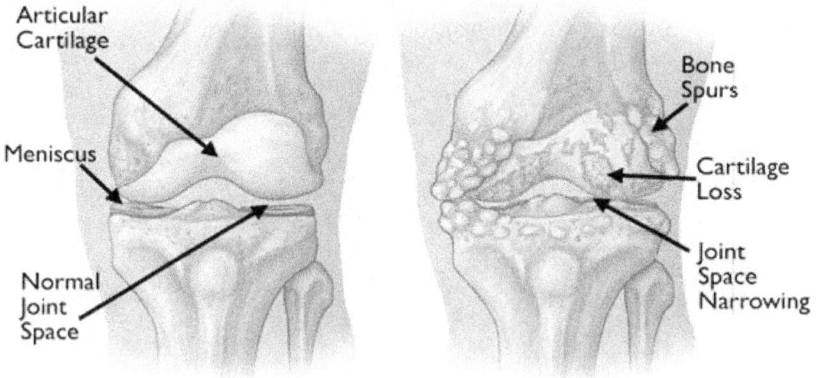


Figure 2: Original Knee & Knee with debris

**Rheumatoid arthritis:** This is a disease in which the synovial membrane that surrounds the joint becomes inflamed and thickened. This chronic inflammation can damage the cartilage and eventually cause cartilage loss, pain, and stiffness. Rheumatoid arthritis is the most common form of a group of disorders termed "inflammatory arthritis."

**Post-traumatic arthritis:** This can follow a serious knee injury. Fractures of the bones surrounding the knee or tears of the knee ligaments may damage the articular cartilage over time, causing knee pain and limiting knee function.

**Description:** A knee replacement (also called knee arthroplasty) might be more accurately termed a knee "resurfacing" because only the surface of the bones are replaced. There are four basic steps to a knee replacement procedure:

1. **Prepare the bone:** The damaged cartilage surfaces at the ends of the femur and tibia are removed along with a small amount of underlying bone.

2. **Position the metal implants:** The removed cartilage and bone is replaced with metal components that recreate the surface of the joint. These metal parts may be cemented or "press-fit" into the bone.

3. **Resurface the patella:** The under surface of the patella (kneecap) is cut and resurfaced with a plastic button. Some surgeons do not resurface the patella, depending upon the case.

4. **Insert a spacer:** A medical-grade plastic spacer is inserted between the metal components to create a smooth gliding surface.

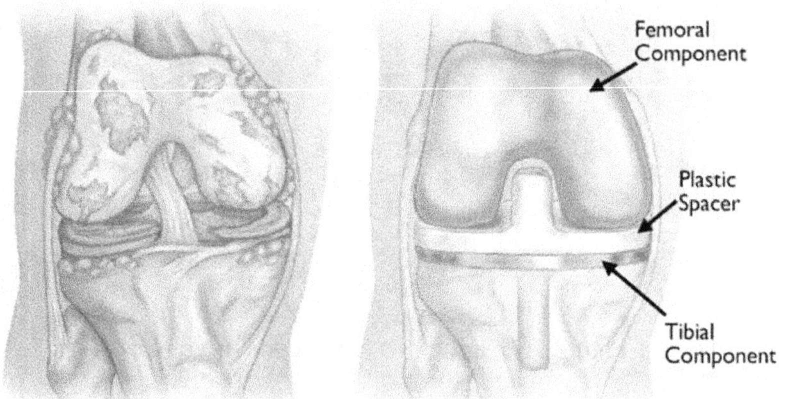


Figure 3: Normal Knee with Knee disease and Total Knee Replacement

**Risk:**

**Infection:** Infection may occur in the wound or deep around the prosthesis. It may happen within days or weeks of your surgery. It may even occur years later. Minor infections in the wound area are generally treated with antibiotics. Major or deep infections may require more surgery and removal of the prosthesis. Any infection in your body can spread to your joint replacement.

**Blood clots:** Blood clots in the leg veins are one of the most common complications of knee replacement surgery. These clots can be life-threatening if they break free and travel to your lungs. Your orthopaedic surgeon will outline a prevention program, which may include periodic elevation of your legs, lower leg exercises to increase circulation, support stockings, and medication to thin your blood.

**Implant problems:** Although implant designs and materials, as well as surgical techniques, continue to advance, implant surfaces may wear down and the components may loosen. Additionally, although an average of 115° of motion is generally anticipated after surgery, scarring of the knee can occasionally occur, and motion may be more limited, particularly in patients with limited motion before surgery.

**Continued pain:** A small number of patients continue to have pain after a knee replacement. This complication is rare, however, and most patients experience excellent pain relief following knee replacement.

**Neurovascular injury:** While rare, injury to the nerves or blood vessels around the knee can occur during surgery.

Knee joint replacement is a surgery to replace a knee joint with a man-made artificial joint. The artificial joint is called a prosthesis. Damaged cartilage and bone are removed from the knee joint. Man-made pieces are then placed in the knee. These pieces may be placed in the following places in the knee joint:

1. **Lower end of the thigh bone** -- This bone is called the femur. The replacement part is usually made of metal.
2. **Upper end of the shin bone, which is the large bone in your lower leg --** This bone is called the tibia. The replacement part is usually made from metal and strong plastic.
3. **Back side of your kneecap** -- Your kneecap is called the patella. The replacement part is usually made from a strong plastic.

You will not feel any pain during the surgery. You will have one of these two types of anaesthesia:

**General anaesthesia** -- This means you will be asleep and unable to feel pain.

**Regional (spinal or epidural) anaesthesia** -- Medicine is put into your back to make you numb below your waist. You will also get medicine to make you sleepy. And you may get medicine that will make you forget about the procedure, even though you are not fully asleep.

After you receive anaesthesia, your surgeon will make a cut over your knee to open it up. This cut is often 8 to 10 inches (20 to 25 centimeters) long. Then your surgeon will:

- Move your kneecap (patella) out of the way, then cut the ends of your thigh bone and shin (lower leg) bone to fit the replacement part.
- Cut the underside of your kneecap to prepare it for the new pieces that will be attached there.
- Fasten the two parts of the prosthesis to your bones. One part will be attached to the end of your thigh bone and the other part will be attached to your shin bone. The pieces can be attached using bone cement or screws.
- Attach the underside of your kneecap. A special bone cement is used to attach this part.
- Repair your muscles and tendons around the new joint and close the surgical cut.

The surgery takes about 2 hours. Most artificial knees have both metal and plastic parts. Some surgeons now use different materials, including metal on metal, ceramic on ceramic, or ceramic on plastic.

## Dental Implant Modalities

### *Dentures*

Dentures are removable false teeth made of acrylic (plastic), nylon or metal. They fit snugly over the gums to replace missing teeth and eliminate potential problems caused by gaps. Gaps left by missing teeth can cause problems with eating and speech, and teeth either side of the gap may grow into the space at an angle. Dentures (false teeth) are synthetic replacements for missing natural teeth. Tooth decay, gum disease, and facial injuries can lead to tooth loss.

Dentures are designed to help fill out your facial profile and improve your appearance. They also make it easier to eat, chew, and speak regularly. Sometimes all the teeth need to be removed and replaced. You may therefore need either:

**Complete dentures (a full set)** – which replace all your upper or lower teeth

**Partial dentures** – which replace just 1 tooth or a few missing teeth

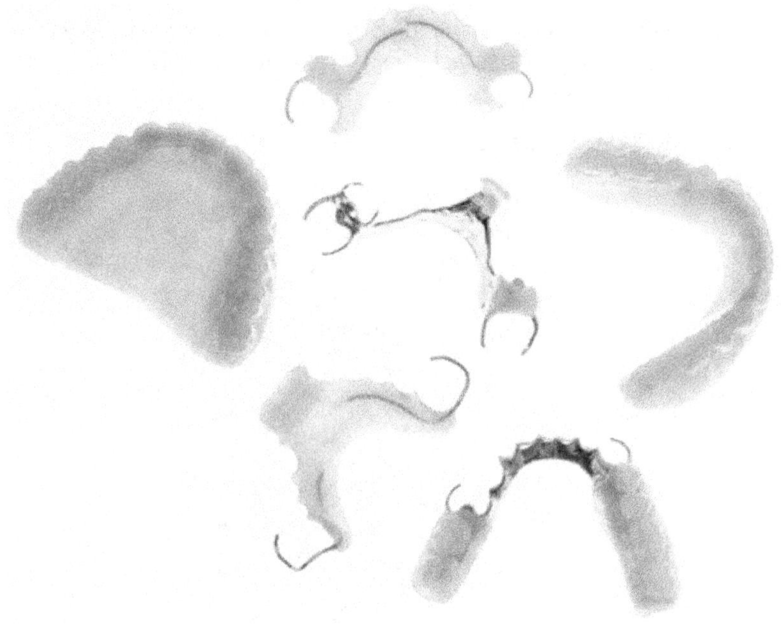

Figure 4: Types of Dentures

Some dentures replace a few missing teeth. Others replace all teeth, gums and surrounding tissues. Tooth loss is the main reason that people get dentures. There are a few primary causes of tooth loss, including:

- **Periodontal disease**
- **Poor oral care**
- **Severe tooth decay**
- **Facial or jaw injury**
- **Infection**

The "fake teeth" in dentures are usually made of plastic or porcelain. The fake "gums" are made of acrylics. The supporting frame of dentures that holds the false teeth in place resembles the natural gum line. There are many different types of dentures available. They come in removable and fixed forms.

**1. Complete Dentures:** Complete dentures are also called full dentures. They're replacements for entire sets of teeth. Most dentists will try to save at least some natural teeth before recommending full dentures. But complete dentures are usually necessary if all other options have been exhausted. Dentures are made of acrylic resin and are only supported by remaining hard and soft tissues. They are not as stable as natural teeth or implants, which are anchored into the bone.

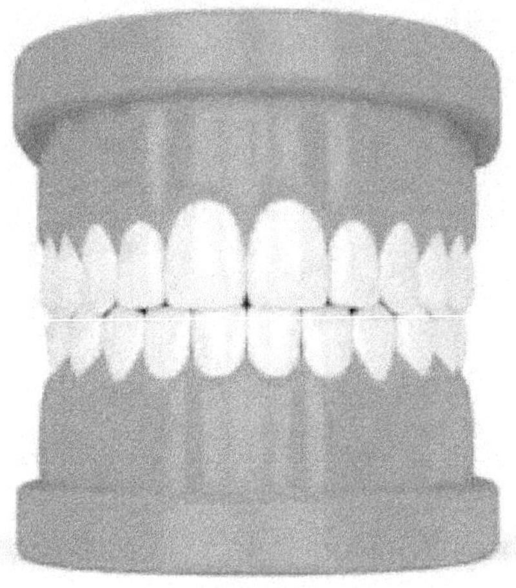

Figure 5: Complete Dentures

**Pros:**

- Restores eating and chewing
- Improves self-esteem and confidence
- Maintains a fuller, more youthful appearance
- Cost-effective

**Cons:**

- Requires maintenance like relines and repairs
- Retention of lower dentures declines over time
- Can slip out of place when speaking or eating
- A lisp may develop

**2. Fixed Partial Dentures (Implant-supported bridge):** Fixed partial dentures (FPD) are also called implant-supported bridges. FPDs replace a few missing teeth in a row with two dental implants and a prosthetic tooth or teeth in between. They are permanently glued or screwed into the mouth. Implant-supported bridges are ideal for patients who have three or more missing teeth in a row. Unlike complete and removable partial false teeth, implant-supported bridges are not removable.

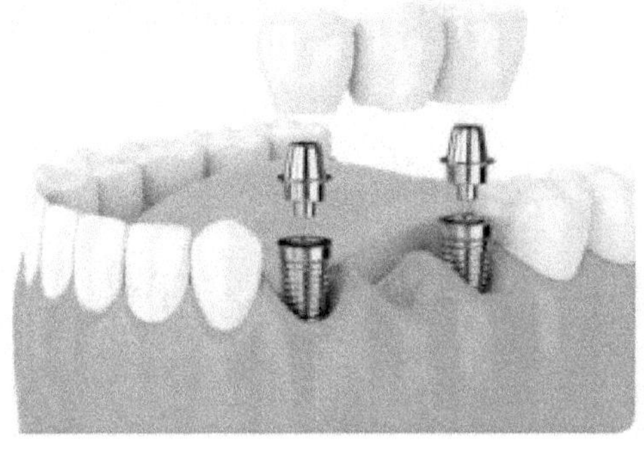

Figure 6: Fixed Partial Dentures

**Pros:**

· Improved aesthetics
· Patients typically feel more secure with fixed (permanent) dentures
· Stronger than removable false teeth
· Consistent tooth positioning and better bite

**Cons:**

· Requires surgery
· Cost is higher than removable dentures
· More difficult to keep clean (requires special floss)

**3. Removable Partial Dentures:** Removable partial dentures (RPD) only replace some missing teeth in your upper or lower jaw. RPDs can be removed at any time and replaced easily. They can restore the natural look, feel, and function of teeth. They consist of false teeth and a gum-colored base that is made of acrylic. The base is attached to two or more clasps that hold the denture in place. Clasps are made of either metal or flexible pink plastic and hook onto the adjacent teeth for increased support.

They are commonly recommended for people who aren't good candidates for an implant-supported bridge. This includes people who can't or don't want to undergo surgery.

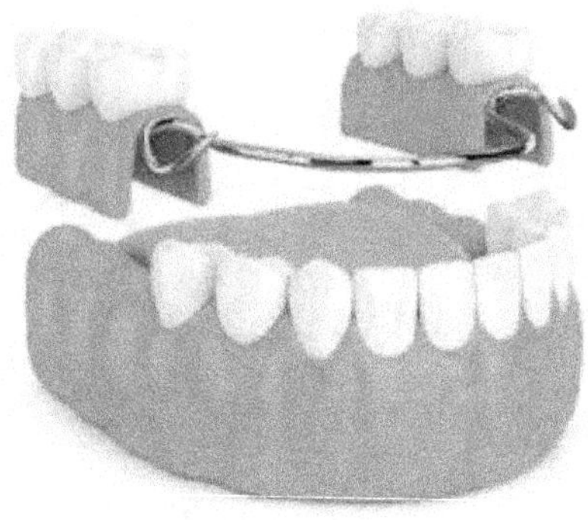

Figure 7: Removable Partial Dentures

**Pros:**

- Durable due to the underlying metal framework
- Easily removable for cleaning
- Don't break easily
- Cost-effective
- Maintain the structural integrity of your mouth (prevent teeth shifting)

**Cons:**

- Can only be used to replace some missing teeth
- Prone to plaque build-up if not cleaned properly
- May have some metal clasps that show when smiling

**4. Implant-Retained Dentures (Overdentures):** An overdenture, also called an implant-supported denture, is held in place on top of your gums by dental implants. Most overdentures are held in place with at least four implants, but this is not always the case. Overdentures can also be placed in the upper jaw, lower jaw, or both. They have more stability and chewing function than conventional dentures. However, you must remove them every night to clean them and allow your gum tissues to rest.

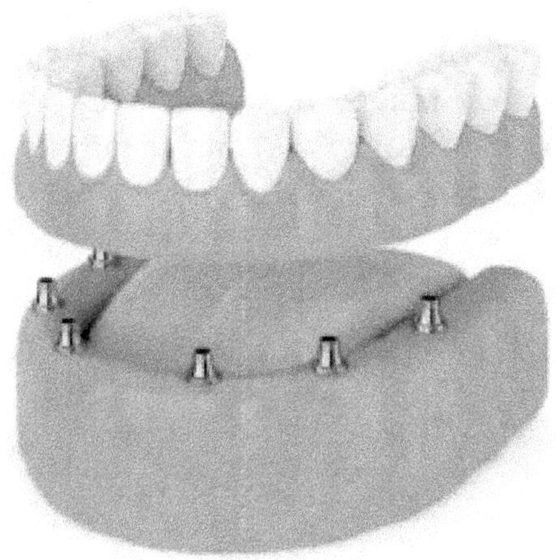

Figure 8: Removable Partial Dentures

**Pros:**

- Stable and robust
- Won't loosen while speaking
- Good chewing ability
- Comfortable, custom fit
- More aesthetically pleasing and natural-looking than traditional dentures

**Cons:**

- Invasive surgery
- Increased treatment time
- Expensive
- May require a bone graft or sinus augmentation to support the denture implants
- Attachments can become loose and require tightening

**5. Immediate Dentures:** After all of your teeth are extracted, you must wait at least 6 to 8 weeks before traditional dentures are placed. This gives your mouth enough time to heal. Removable immediate dentures are placed directly after your natural teeth are extracted. Although convenient, immediate dentures are more challenging than traditional dentures because they are not molded to your gums. They also don't look as natural and require more upkeep. Immediate dentures are also ideal for patients who have sensitive gums and teeth. The denture can be worn for a few weeks before placing a permanent denture to provide a smoother transition.

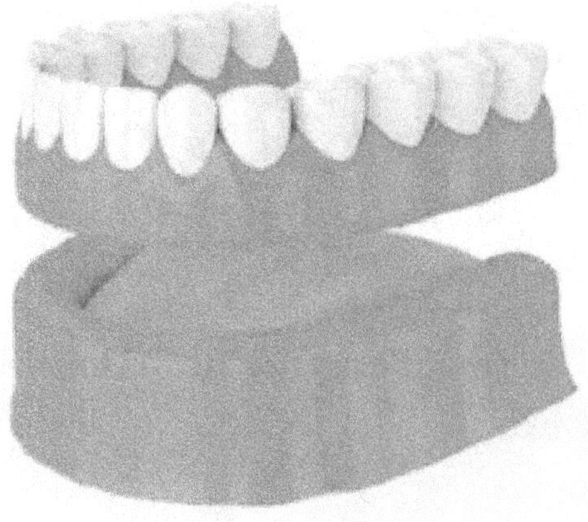

Figure 9: Immediate Dentures

**Pros:**

- Provide a temporary solution for eating and talking after getting teeth extracted
- Allow you to have teeth while your mouth is healing, reducing the amount of time you don't have teeth
- Serves as a bandaid to help extraction sites heal, minimizing swelling and bleeding

**Cons:**

- Not a long-term solution
- Not as natural looking as permanent dentures
- Prone to breakage and bacteria build-up
- Requires multiple adjustments and, eventually, reline or replacement

**6. All-on-4 Implant Dentures:** All-On-4 implant dentures are ideal for patients who need a complete set of dentures. They replace all of your missing teeth in the upper and/or lower jaws using four dental implants. You cannot take the denture out by yourself, but your dentist can remove it.

**Pros:**

- More durable than traditional complete dentures
- More natural-looking than implant supported dentures
- Dentists can place temporary prostheses on the same day as the implant procedure

**Cons:**

- Dentists are the only ones who can remove them
- Requires diet restrictions during the first three months until the final prosthesis is placed
- More expensive than traditional dentures

**7. Economy Dentures:** Dentists do not recommend economy dentures because they can harm your mouth and lead to poor oral hygiene. Economy dentures are a premade, generic, and inexpensive type of denture. They are not custom-made for your mouth. A denture adhesive is also necessary to keep the dentures in place.

**Pros:**

- More affordable than other types of dentures
- Easily accessible

**Cons:**

- Unnatural looking
- Less secure due to needing denture adhesive
- Can cause more harm to your oral health

## *Types of Dental Implants*

There are three types of implants like following:

1. Endosteal Implants
2. Transosteal Implants
3. Subperiosteal Implants

**1. Endosteal Implants:** In this type, the tooth roots are replaced by screws, cylinders, or blades that are usually made of titanium or ceramic material. The implant is surgically drilled into the jawbone that helps to hold the artificial teeth in place. Thus, these implants lie completely inside the jawbone, well below the gums. However, artificial teeth are not directly connected to endosteal implants. So, once the dental implant is inserted into the jawbone, a post is connected to the implant. The artificial tooth is then securely placed over the post.

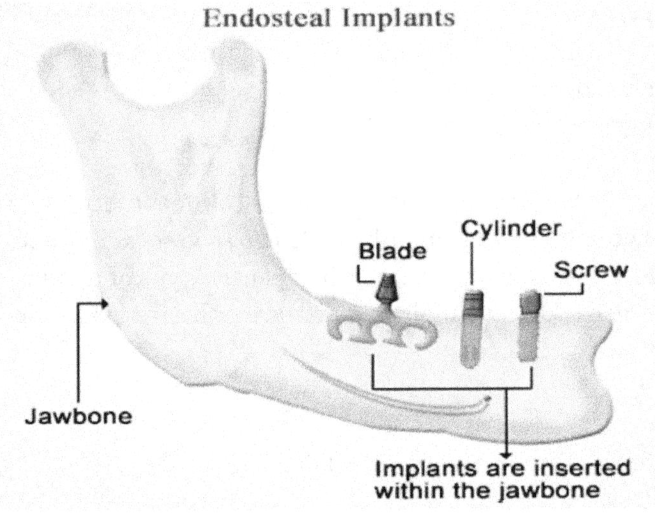


Figure 10: Endosteal Dental Implant

**2.Transosteal Implants:** These implants that can be fitted only to the lower jawbone are generally not recommended as the surgical procedure is complicated and extensive. The procedure involves attaching a metal plate at the bottom of the jawbone, with screws running through the jawbone, and the posts embedded within the gum tissue.

An incision is made below the chin to fix the plate with screws and posts on top, to attach the artificial teeth. However, these implants are not available at a pocket-friendly price as they have to be customized according to the width and height of the jawbone. This will ensure that the implant fits correctly on the individual.

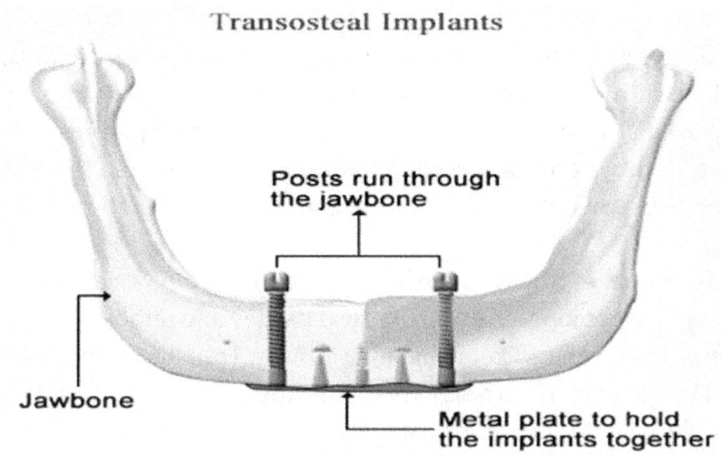


Figure 11: Transosteal Dental Implant

**3. Subperiosteal Implants:** A metal framework is firmly secured on the jawbone, but the framework lies below the gum line. Metal posts are again necessary, and appear to be projecting outwards above the gum line through the metal frame. The procedure is time-consuming, has minimal success rate, and can result in post-surgical scars.

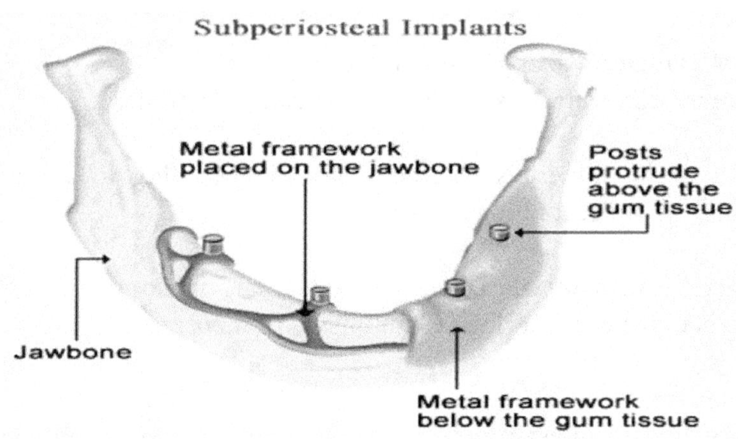


Figure 12: Subperiosteal Dental Implant

## *Dental filling materials*

**Dental fillings** are single or combinations of metals, plastics, glass or other materials used to repair or restore teeth. One of the most popular uses of fillings is to "fill" an area of tooth that your dentist has removed due to decay – "a cavity." Fillings are also used to repair cracked or broken teeth and teeth that have been worn down from misuse (such as from nail-biting or tooth grinding).

**Requirements of filling materials:**
1. Biologically compatible with natural tissues in contact
2. Mimic the tooth in: Color shape & stability, Translucency, Coefficient of thermal expansion & Hardness (wear resistant)
3. Should bond to the tooth structure
4. Have mechanical properties enough to withstand the force
5. Should be dimensionally stable
6. Not to be degradable in oral fluids
7. Easily repair if fractured
8. Easily finished & polished
9. Inexpensive & have long shell life
10. Should be radiopaque (white in x-rays)

Tooth filling materials can be classified according to metallic materials and non-metallic materials.

1. **Metallic materials:** Gold & Amalgam
2. **Non-metallic materials:** Cement, Composite & Ceramics

Tooth filling materials can be classified according to direct filling materials and indirect filling materials.

1. **Direct filling materials:** Direct gold foil, Amalgam, Composite & Cement
2. **Indirect filling materials:** Gold inlays, Composite inlays & Ceramic inlays

Tooth filling materials can be classified according to posterior filling materials and anterior filling materials.

1. **Posterior filling materials:** Gold, Amalgam, Composite & Ceramics
2. **Anterior filling materials:** Cement, Ceramics & Composites

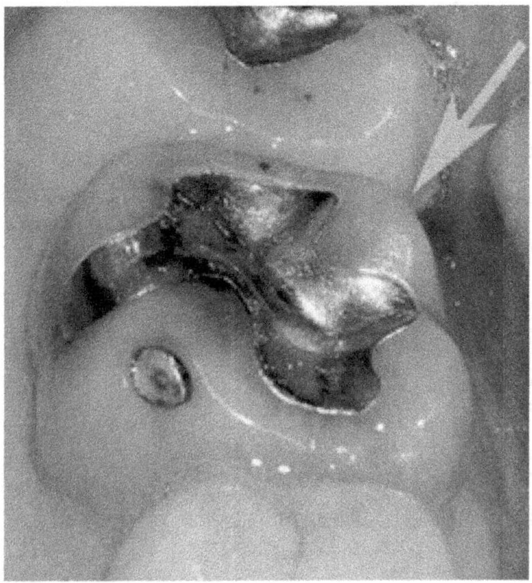

Figure 13: Dental filling material

## *Dental restoration material*

Dental restorative materials are specially fabricated materials designed to restore the function, integrity and morphology of missing tooth structure, usually resulting from, but not limited to dental caries.

**Classification:**

**Temporary, Intermediate & Permanent:**

- Zinc oxide Eugenol- Temporary
- Polymer reinforced cement & Improved ZOE-Intermediate
- Direct filling gold, Amalgam, Composite, Porcelain, Cast material inlays-Permanent

**Direct & Indirect:**

- Amalgam, Composite, direct filling gold- Direct

- Porcelain, Composite & Cast metal inlays- Indirect

**Esthetic & Non-esthetic:**

- Composite, Porcelain- Esthetic
- Amalgam, direct filling gold, cast metal inlays- Non esthetic

**1) Amalgam:** Amalgam is a metal alloy of which one of the element is mercury (Hg). Alloys are metals that are a combination of several elements. It is classified according to:

- Based on copper content: High copper (13-30%), Low copper (<6%)
- Based on zinc content: Zinc containing (>0.01%) , Zinc free (<0.01%)
- Based on size of alloy: Microcut, Macrocut
- Based on shape of the alloy particle: Spherical, Spheroidal and Lathe cut
- Based on no. of alloyed metals: Binary alloys (silver-tin), Ternary alloys (silver-tin-copper) and Quaternary (silver-tin-copper-indium)

**Advantages:**

- Inexpensive
- Easy to Use
- Technique Insensitive
- Durable

**Disadvantages:**

- Non-adhesive
- Requires Mechanical retention
- Poor esthetics
- Environmental & Occupational Hazards

**2) Composites:** Restorative material composed of two phases: Matrix & Filler bound together by coupling agents. Further divided into Macro-filled (70-80% filler), Micro-filled (40-50% filler) & Hybrid (75-80% filler).

**Advantages:**

- Adhesive

- Reasonable wear properties
- Minimal tooth preparation required
- Micromechanical bond to enamel

**Disadvantages:**

- Expensive
- Time consuming
- Sensitive

**3)Others:** Dental cements: Zinc Phosphate, Zinc Polycarboxylate, Calcium hydroxide cement are used as a Restorative materials.

**Choices of Appropriate Restorative Material:** The choice of material mainly depends on:

- Location & extent of carries
- Age & Gender of Patient
- Strength of material desired
- Allergy to specific material
- Economic factors

# Dental impression material

A dental impression is defined as the negative record of the tissues of the mouth. It is used to reproduce the form of the teeth & surrounding tissues.

**Properties of an Impression material:**

1. Have pleasant taste, odor & esthetic color.
2. Not contain any toxic or irritating ingredients.
3. Be economical.
4. Have adequate shelf life for storage & distribution.
5. Be easy to use with minimum equipments.
6. Stability
7. Have adequate strength so that it will not break or tear while removing from mouth

| Mode of Setting | Rigid | Elastic |
|---|---|---|
| Set by chemical reaction | Impression plaster, zinc oxide eugenol | Polysulfide, Polyether, Silicone |
| Set by temperature change | Compound, waxes | Ager hydrocolloid |

Table 1: Mode of settings used in Dental impression materials

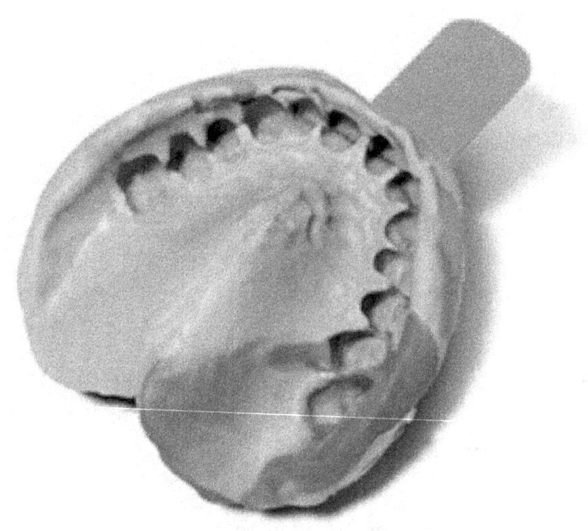

Figure 14: Dental impression

## *Manufacturing Process of Orthopedic & Dental Implant*

An Orthopedic & Dental Implant is a medical device produced to supplant in the spot of a missing joint, issue or tooth that remains to be worked out a harmed bone or tissue. Process of orthopaedic & Dental implants manufacturing is fundamentally created utilizing treated steel and titanium amalgams for quality and the covering that are done with plastic or ceramic.

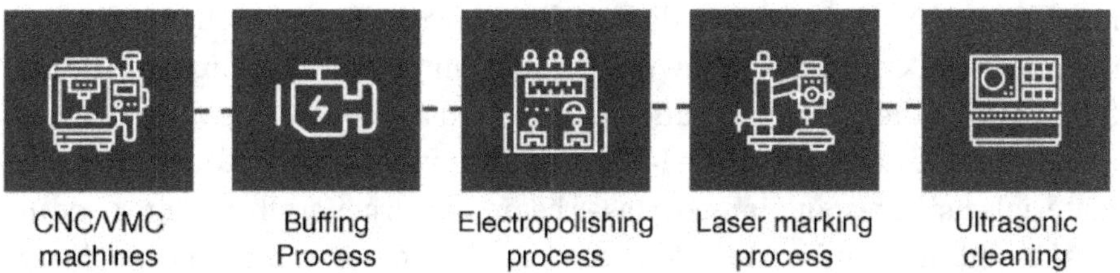


Figure 15: Manufacturing Process of Orthopedic & Dental Implant

**Materials used:**
Implant Material
**Metals:**

1. Titanium
2. Titanium Alloy
3. Stainless steel

**Orthopedic & Dental implants making process/machinery (CNC/VMC Machine):** CNC machining is the manufacturing procedure where pre-modified programming computers software dictates the movements of factory tools and machinery. The procedure can be utilized to control the scope of complex machineries, from processors and machines to plants and switches. With CNC machining, the three-dimensional cutting undertaking can be cultivated in a solitary arrangement of prompts.

VMC the Vertical Machine is preferred where three-axis works are done on a single face as in molding and die work. Vertical machining occurs on a vertical machining center, (VMC), which employs a spindle with a vertical orientation. With a vertically oriented spindle, tools stick straight down from the tool holder and often cut across the top of a workpiece.

**Buffing Process:** Buffing process is used to shine the metal, or any composites by the use of a cloth wheel soaked with cutting compounds or rouges. The buffing cloth holds the compound, by the time the compound does the cutting. The industry names this as the "polishing" process. Buffing normally requires two things, a cutting buff and a finishing buff. The cutting buff, which is the roughest buffing operation is good for removing pits, polishing lines or scratches.

**Electro polishing Process:** Electro polishing process also called as the electrochemical polishing, is a process that removes material from a metallic workpiece it reduces the roughness from the surface by levelling up the micro-peaks and the hollowness improvising the surface finish. It is used for polishing the metal parts and is also stated as the electroplating.

**Laser making Process:** The laser marking process is used for marking the materials using a spot diameter laser beam and is generally used for adding marks and or brand names. A laser beam is used on a material to change and colour it.

**Ultrasonic Cleaning:** Ultrasonic cleaners are improving productivity in modern purifying for about 70 years; it\'s simply developed progressively compelling and solid over the long haul.

# VII

# Biocompatibility and Sterilization

## Methods for testing and evaluating biocompatibility

### *Introduction*

**Biocompatibility** is, by definition, a measurement of how compatible a device or material is with a biological system. The ISO 10993-1: 2018 standard defines biocompatibility as the "ability of a medical device or material to perform with an appropriate host response in a specific application".

The purpose of performing biocompatibility testing is to determine the fitness of a device for human use, and to see whether use of the device can have any potentially harmful physiological effects. As stated by the International Organization of Standards (ISO): "The primary aim of this part of ISO 10993 is the protection of humans from potential risks arising from the use of medical devices." (ISO 10993-1:2018).

Before performing biocompatibility testing, it is important for the manufacturer to gain a better understanding of the device materials, device manufacturing, sterilization and other processes. The ISO 10993-1:2018 standard emphasizes chemical characterization before proceeding to in vitro and in vivo biocompatibility testing.

The general process of biocompatibility testing can be broken up into three steps: planning, testing and evaluating the data. In the planning stage data on the materials used to manufacture the device should be collected. A biological evaluation plan (BEP) should also be developed which will determine the type of testing that is required. Testing typically starts with in vitro screening by performing cytotoxicity testing. Extractable leachable testing, or chemical characterization, is also usually conducted before the in vivo testing.

## Cytotoxicity in VITRO-ISO 10993-5

Cytotoxicity is a biocompatibility test performed on mammalian cells in culture. There are three in vitro cytotoxicity tests that performs: MEM Elution, Agarose Overlay, and Direct Contact. Cytotoxicity testing evaluates the toxicity or materials and chemicals by exposing cultured cells to the sample directly or by preparing an extract from the sample and exposing the cells to the extract.

## Hemolysis Testing- ASTM F756

Hemolysis tests, can be done via direct and extract methods, to evaluate the adverse effects of medical devices, leachable, and biomaterials on rabbit blood. This assay is well suited to evaluate the hemocompatibility of medical devices and biomaterials according to the international standard ISO 10993-4:2017 and ASTM F756.

## In VIVO Biocompatibility Testing

Once in vitro testing has been completed, in vivo biological testing is performed, with the extent of type of testing to be performed based upon the device's intended use. In vivo testing can range from skin irritation testing, to sensitization testing, implantation testing and systemic toxicity testing. Turnaround time for tests can range from three weeks to greater than several months, depending on the specific test data needed.

## Hemocompatibility

Materials used in blood contacting devices (e.g. intravenous catheters, hemodialysis sets, blood transfusion sets, vascular prostheses) must be assessed for blood compatibility to establish their safety. In practice, all materials are to some degree incompatible with blood because they can either disrupt the blood cells (hemolysis) or activate the coagulation pathways (thrombogenicity) and/or the complement system.

The hemolysis assay is recommended for all devices or device materials except those which contact only intact skin or mucous membranes. This test measures the damage to red blood cells when they are exposed to materials or their extracts, and compares it to positive and negative controls.

Coagulation assays measure the effect of the test article on human blood coagulation time. They are recommended for all devices with blood contact. The Prothrombin Time Assay (PT) is a general screening test for the detection of coagulation abnormalities in the extrinsic pathway. The Partial Thromboplastin Time Assay (PTT) detects coagulation abnormalities in the intrinsic pathway.

The most common test for thrombogenicity is the in vivo method. For devices unsuited to this test method, ISO 10993-4 requires tests in each of four categories: coagulation, platelets, hematology, and complement system.

Complement activation testing is recommended for implant devices that contact circulatory blood. This in vitro assay measures complement activation in human plasma as a result of exposure of the plasma to the test article or an extract. The measure of complement actuation indicates whether a test article is capable of inducing a complement-induced inflammatory immune response in humans.

Other blood compatibility tests and specific in vivo studies may be required to complete the assessment of material-blood interactions, especially to meet ISO requirements.

## *Osteocompatibility*

Cell culture assays are used to assess the biocompatibility of a material or extract through the use of isolated cells in vitro. These techniques are useful in evaluating the toxicity or irritancy potential of materials and chemicals. They provide an excellent way to screen materials prior to in vivo tests.

These tests estimate the local irritation potential of devices, materials or extracts, using sites such as skin or mucous membranes, usually in an animal model. The route of exposure (skin, eye, mucosa) and duration of contact should be analogous to the anticipated clinical use of the device, but it is often prudent to exaggerate exposure conditions somewhat to establish a margin of safety for patients.

In the Intracutaneous Test, extracts of the test material and blanks are injected intradermally. The injection sites are scored for erythema and edema (redness and swelling). This procedure is recommended for devices that will have externally communicating or internal contact with the body or body fluids. It reliably detects the potential for local irritation due to chemicals that may be extracted from a biomaterial.

The Primary Skin Irritation test should be considered for topical devices that have external contact with intact or breached skin. In this procedure, the test material or an extract is applied directly to intact and abraded sites on the skin of a rabbit. After a 24-hour exposure, the material is removed and the sites are scored for erythema and edema.

## *Tissue response to external materials*

Tissue response represents an important feature in biocompatibility in implant procedures. Biomaterials are the biological or synthetic materials that are used to restore a part of a living system and/or to maintain contact with living tissue. The local and systemic responses of the tissue represent an important feature of biocompatibility. And described the term, biocompatibility, as the ability of a biomaterial, prosthesis, or medical device to perform with an appropriate host response in a specific application.

The fundamental characteristics of tissue response after implantation of the biomaterials are injury, blood material interactions, provisional matrix formation, acute and chronic inflammation, granulation tissue formation, foreign body reaction, and fibrous capsule development.

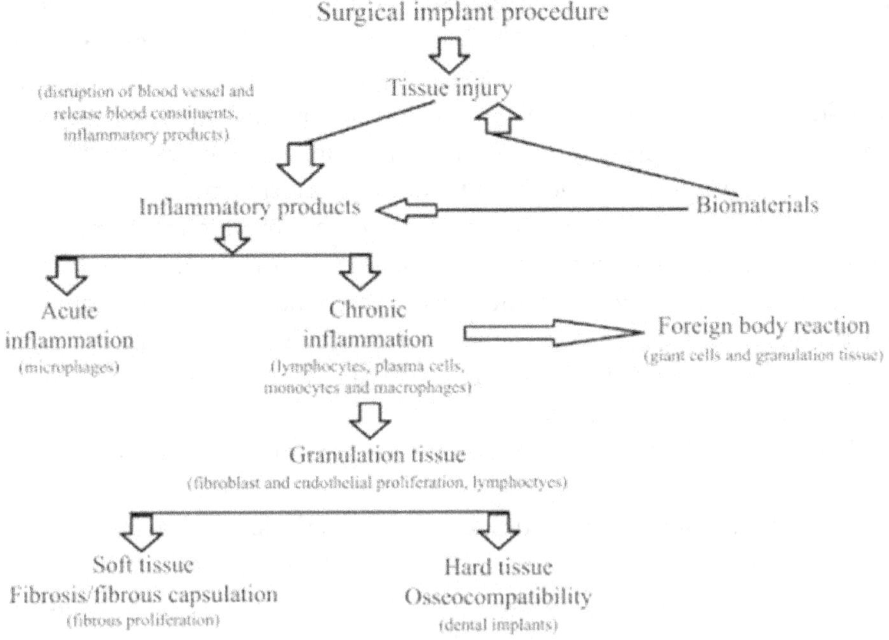



Figure 1: Tissue response to external materials

An injury begins from the surgical intervention process of implantation and continues postoperatively. Tissue injury predisposes blood vessel disruption with concomitant release of blood constituents.

Immediately after the injury, the alterations in the vascular flow and permeability occur, thus initiating the inflammatory response by the escape of blood cells, fluids, and proteins from the vascular component. The injury and perturbation of homeostatic mechanism lead to the cellular cascades of the healing process.

The initial acute inflammatory response is activated by injury to the vascular component of the tissue and the blood material interactions.

Provisional matrix formation at the implant site is formed immediately after the injury of vascularized tissue. The provisional matrix is composed of inflammatory cells, fibrin, and endothelial cells. The mitogens, chemokines, cytokines, and growth factors are released in the provisional matrix and influence wound healing process.

The components of the provisional matrix initiate the resolution, reorganization, and repair processes. During the process of acute inflammation, the major function of the neutrophils/microphages is to phagocytose microbes and foreign materials. The engulfment and degradation of biomaterial may or may not occur and is greatly dependent on the property of the biomaterial. Generally, biomaterials are not engulfed by microphages/macrophages because of the size disparity.

In certain biomaterials, phagocytosis may occur in which they are coated by natural substances, such as serum factors, known as opsonins. These opsonins are recognized by the host tissue and provoke degradation. Furthermore, this degradation process does not involve engulfment of the biomaterial but results in the extracellular release of leukocyte products in an attempt to degrade the biomaterial.

The neutrophils release enzymes, the amount of which depends on the size of the biomaterial particle, thus suggesting that activation of inflammatory response in the tissue depends on the size of the implant and the material of the implant, which is phagocytosable or nonphagocytosable. Persistent inflammation at the tissue injury of the implanted site results in chronic inflammation.

The formation of the granulation tissue is considered a hallmark of the healing inflammation process. The initiation of granulation tissue formation depends on the site and size of the tissue injury, the formation of which can be anticipated in 3 to 5 days of the implantation. Foreign body reaction is characterized by foreign body giant cells and granulation tissue components.

The physical and chemical properties of the biomaterial used, however, determine the composition of the foreign body reaction. Anderson mentions that foreign body reaction in the implant site might be controlled by the surface properties of the biomaterial, form of the implant, and relationship between the surface area of the biomaterial and the volume of the implant. Foreign body reaction with granulation tissue development is considered a normal wound healing response to the implanted biomaterials.

## Biodegradable materials and their applications

Biodegradable materials, by definition, change their chemical and potentially physical form upon contact with the biological environment. There are two distinct stages to the biodegradation process, especially in bulk degradation. The first stage is restricted to the random cleavage of molecular linkages. The resulting decrease in molecular weight produces some change in mechanical properties and morphology, but no weight loss.

The second stage involves a measurable weight loss in addition to chain cleavage. It begins when the molecular weight of the polymer has decreased to the point that chain scission produces oligomers that are small enough to solubilize and diffuse out from the network. Biodegradable materials can find applications as temporary implants (e.g., stents or orthopedic screws or wires), surgical sutures, and also in tissue engineering or drug delivery.

The performance of permanent biomedical implants (e.g., total joint replacements, fracture fixation devices, artificial heart valves) can be affected by issues related to inflammation, thrombus formation, stress shielding, and subsequent device removal surgeries.

Other disadvantages of permanent biomedical devices are long-term migration of permanent implants, fracture-induced pain, as well as interferences stemming from the use of magnetic fields of the material with standard imaging equipment are typically operational in the body for many years or even decades since they are meant to replace or repair function of an anatomical body part.

When a biomedical implant is meant to be only temporary, the time that the biodegradable biomaterial will be designed to be present in the body will be highly dependent on the type of tissue where the repair or replacement is located. For example, for bone, a device needs to mechanically support healing for at least 6 weeks, after which slow degradation of the biomaterial is desired to occur at a velocity that is as close as possible to that of new bone synthesis.

In other applications, such as drug delivery, the degradation needs to be designed in such a way that the drug is released in a timely manner at the right anatomical location, and this time can vary from minutes or hours to days.

At the same time, biodegradable materials can be used in tissue engineering, mainly as scaffolds guiding the formation of new tissue or organs. For tissue engineering, biodegradable scaffolds are porous to allow cell migration.

Next, cells work to produce new tissue, while the biodegradable scaffold slowly dissolves and gives way for the new tissue to form in its place. It is useful to define three different terms that are often used: biodegradable, bioresorbable, and bioabsorbable.

Most biomaterials discussed here are biodegradable. That is, these are materials that are able to break down, or degrade, when either partially or fully exposed to the physiological environment, where a biological agent (such as an enzyme) is responsible for the degradation. This term should not be confused with "bioresorbable." A certain material is bioresorbable in the context of biological reactions, such as bone resorption by osteoclasts, and has the ability to grow back.

Since artificial biomaterials are not living tissues, they lack the potential of regrowth and are thus biodegradable but not bioresorbable. Bioabsorbable refers to how biodegradation products of a foreign material are affected by the host metabolic processes. Often sutures are called absorbable, and they tend to be absorbed after approximately 90 to 120 days. For temporary biomedical implants, it is a desirable direction to substitute biomedical polymers or alloys that are used in functional vascular and orthopedic implants with biodegradable biomaterials.

## Sterilization Process

**Sterilization:** A Physical or chemical process that completely destroys or removes all microbial life, including spores.

**Disinfection:** It is killing or removing of harmful microorganisms.

**Disinfectant:** Produces used to kill microorganisms or inanimate objects or surfaces. Disinfectants are not necessarily sporicidal, but may be sporostatic, inhibiting germination or outgrowth.

**Antiseptic:** A product that destroys or inhibits the growth of microorganisms in or on living tissue.

**Aseptic:** Characterized by the absence of pathogenic microbes.

The process of making some substances free from living bacteria or other microorganisms. All implants require sterilization.

Some methods of sterilization can lead to polymer spoilage. In dry heat sterilization the temperature varies between 160° to 190° C, above the melting and softening temperature of many linear polymers such as polyethylene and polymethylmethacrylate, so sterilization of this polymer by heat is unsuitable.

In the case of polyamide (nylon), oxidation will be observed at dry sterilization temperatures, although it is below its melting temperature. Steam sterilization is performed at relatively low temperatures (120-135°C) under high steam pressure.

Chemical agents such as ethylene and propylene oxide gases and phenolic and hypo chloride solutions are widely used to sterilize polymers as they can be used at low temperatures. Chemical sterilization takes longer than the above heating methods and is more expensive.

Polymer spoilage also occurs when chemical agents are sterilized at room temperature. Most of polymeric implants can be sterilized with this method.

Radiation sterilization using isotope cobalt 60 also degrades the polymer as polymer chains can be broken and rearranged at high doses. In the case of polyethylene, at high doses (above 106 g) it becomes a brittle, hard material. This is due to the combination of random chain skiing and crosslinking. Sterilization can be accomplished by an amalgamation of heat, chemicals, irradiation, high pressure and filtration such as steam under pressure, dry heat, ultraviolet radiation, gas vapour sterilants, chlorine dioxide gas etc. Successful sterilization strategies are necessary for working in a lab and negligence of this could lead to severe consequences, it could unexpectedly cost a life.

The Sterilization is conveyed out by the methods according to requirement. The methods are: 1. Moist Heat Sterilization 2. Dry Heat Sterilization 3. Gas Sterilization and others.

**1. Moist Heat Sterilization:** Moderate pressure is utilized in steam sterilization. Steam is utilized under pressure as a means of accomplishing an elevated temperature. It is dominant to confirm the accurate quality of steam is utilized in order to keep away the problems which follow, superheating of the steam, failure of steam penetration into porous loads, incorrect removal of air, etc.

**2.Dry Heat Sterilization:** Dry heat sterilization is utilized for heat-stable non-aqueous preparations, powders and definite impregnated dressings. It may also be utilized for sterilization of some types of container. Sterilization by dry heat is generally carried out in a hot-air oven. Heat is carried from its source to load by radiation, convention and to a small extent by conduction.

This process can eliminate heat-resistant endotoxin. In each cycle it is predominant to make sure that the entire content of each container is maintained for a successful blend of time and temperature for most part to allow temperature variations in hot-air ovens, which may be considerable. Dry heat is utilized to sterilize glassware, porcelain and metal equipment, oils and fats and powders i.e. talc, etc.

**3. Gas Sterilization:** Gaseous sterilizing agents are of two main types, oxidizing and alkylating agents. Vapour phase hydrogen peroxide is an example of the former. Ethylene oxide and formaldehyde are instance of the alkylating agents. However, the BP states that gaseous sterilization is used when there is no acceptable replacement. The main advantage of ethylene oxide is that many types of materials, including thermo labile materials, can be sterilized without damage.

Low temperature steam with formaldehyde has been utilized as an option for sterilizing thermo labile substances. Both ethylene oxide and formaldehyde have health risks and strict monitoring of personnel revealed to the gases required to make sure protection from harmful effects.

**4.Sterilization by Radiation:** Radiations can be split up into two groups: electromagnetic waves and streams of particulate matter. The former group consists infrared radiation, ultraviolet light, X-rays and gamma rays. The latter group includes alpha and beta radiations. More frequently infrared radiation, ultraviolet light, gamma radiation and high-velocity electrons are utilized for sterilization.

1. **Ultraviolet Light:** A narrow range of UV wavelength is successful in eliminating the microorganism. The wavelength is powerfully absorbed by the nucleoproteins. The most important disadvantage of UV radiation as a sterilizing agent is its poor penetrating power. This is the result of powerful absorption by many substances. The application of UV radiation is limited.

2. **Ionizing Radiations:** Ionizing radiations are satisfactory for commercial sterilization processes. It must have good penetrating power, high sterilizing efficiency, little or no damage result on irradiated materials and are capable of being produced efficiently. The radiations that satisfy these four measures are best high-speed electrons from machines and gamma rays from radioactive isotopes.

**5. Sterilization by Filtration:** Membrane filters are built from cellulose derives or other polymers. There are no loose fibres or molecules in membrane filters. They keep molecules bigger than the pore size on the filter surface hence filters particularly useful in noticing of small numbers of bacteria.

Passage through a filter of suitable pore size can remove bacteria and moulds. Viruses and mycoplasma may not be maintained. After filtration the liquid is aseptically dispensed into formerly sterilized containers which are later sealed.

Other than this, it is tough to make universal statements about the various methods of sterilization because there can be huge non-identical in these considerations depending on the size and location of the sterilizer, as well as the methods waged for product release.

## Types of Sterilizer

## *1. ETO Sterilization:*

ETO stands for Ethylene oxide sterilization. Ethylene oxide sterilization is a type of chemical process consisting of four primary variables namely gas concentration, humidity, temperature and time.

Ethylene oxide is an alkylation agent that disrupts DNA of microorganisms which prevents them from reproducing. ETO sterilization assures that a safe and sterile product will be delivered to the market each and every time.

World / industries have been praising sterilization by steam & superlative for destroying bacteria, fungi and spores. Steam sterilization is also most cost effective & easy to use method available but steam is not applicable to all materials and instruments. Advancement in medical procedures has resulted in the increased usage of delicate instruments which can't be steam sterilized as they cannot survive excessive temperatures or moisture of steam. So Heat and moisture sensitive equipment require alternative methods of sterilization. And that is where ETO Sterilization is used.

ETO gas is carcinogenic, explosive and mutagenic. Ethylene Oxide (ETO) is a common gas used for low temperature sterilization. It is a colorless, poisonous gas that attacks the cellular proteins and nucleic acids of microorganisms. It is most commonly used to sterilize instruments with long lumens such as endoscopes and all materials that have to be sterilized but cannot withstand higher temperature. ETO process temperatures from 25 - 55°C are used. A lower temperature results in a less efficient process which leads to a longer exposure time. ETO Sterilizer is equipment, which facilitate ETO Sterilization process. ETO Sterilizers are available in various capacities from 0.45m3 to 44m3 volumetric capacities to carry out ETO

Sterilization.

Figure 2: ETO Sterilizer

There are three phase in ETO Sterilizer:

- Preconditioning
- Sterilization
- Aeration (Degassing) Cycle time is usually more than 14 hours.

**Advantages of ETO Sterilization:**

1. Low temperature
2. High efficiency – destroys micro-organisms including resistant spores
3. Large sterilizing volume/ chamber capacity
4. Non corrosive to: plastic, metal and rubber materials

**Disadvantages of ETO Sterilization:**

1. Excessively Long cycle
2. Safety concerns - carcinogenic to humans
3. Toxicity issues - toxic residues on surgical instruments and tubing
4. Not recommended for flexible scope
5. ETO is flammable

6. Requires special room conditions, safety equipment and separate ventilation system
7. Relatively high annual costs for maintenance, servicing and consumables.

## 2. *Radiation Sterilization:*

Commercial radiation sterilization has existed since the late 1950s and has grown tremendously in popularity over the last 60 years. Radiation sterilization relies on ionizing radiation, primarily gamma, X-ray or electron radiation, to deactivate microorganisms such as bacteria, fungi, viruses and spores. Due to numerous advantages over heat or chemical based sterilization techniques, this method is particularly attractive in medicine and healthcare-related fields.

Radiation can be lethal to biological organisms by inducing genetic damage and chemical changes in key biological macromolecules.

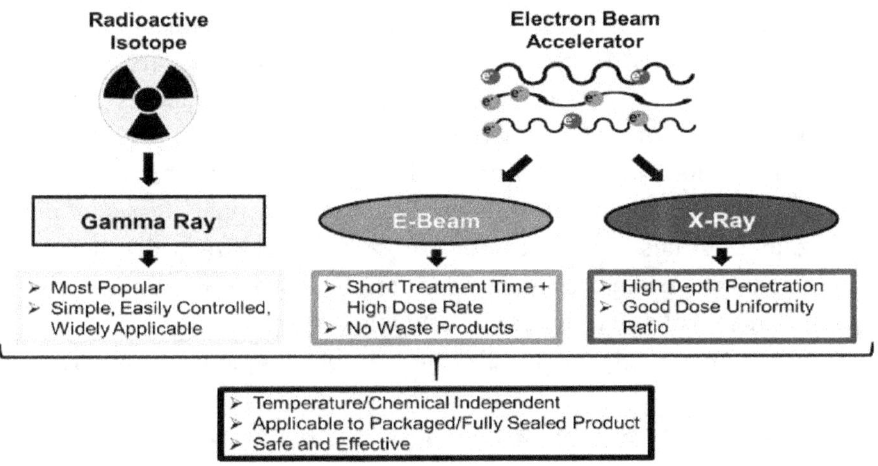


Figure 3: Radiation Sterilizer

During sterilization treatment, the sample of interest is bombarded with high energy electrons or high energy electromagnetic radiation, which leads to the formation of extremely unstable free radicals, molecular ions and secondary electrons. These radiation products then react with nearby molecules to fracture and alter chemical bonds. Incomplete repair of DNA damage ultimately leads to loss of genetic information and cell death. Thus, radiation can kill harmful microorganisms and be used as a sterilization technique.

Three forms of radiation commonly used for commercial radiation sterilization include **gamma radiation, electron beam (e-beam) radiation and X-ray radiation** (Fig.).

**Advantages of radiation based sterilization:** Radiation based sterilization methods offer numerous advantages over traditional chemical or heat-based sterilization:

1. **Terminal Processing:** Due to the penetration depth of ionizing radiation, products can be processed in their fully sealed, final packaging. This limits risk of contamination following sterilization.
2. **Cold Method/Temperature Independence:** Temperature increases during treatment are minimal. Furthermore, radiation sterilization has no heat dependence and is efficient at both ambient temperature and sub-zero temperatures. It is compatible with temperature sensitive materials, such as pharmaceuticals and biological samples.
3. **Chemical Independence:** No volatile or toxic chemicals are needed. In the case of X-ray or e-beam irradiation, no end products requiring disposal are generated during the procedure.
4. **No residue:** Radiation leaves no residue on the sterilized product.
5. **Flexibility:** Radiation can sterilize products of any phase (gaseous, liquid or solid materials), products with variable density, size or thickness, and homogeneous or heterogeneous systems. Furthermore, sterilization can be conducted at any temperature and any pressure.
6. **Time efficiency:** E-beam sterilization can be completed within seconds to minutes.
7. **Sterility assurance level (SAL):** Radiation treatment can yield a high SAL of 10-6 or better, ensuring that less than one out of a million microorganisms survive the sterilization procedure.
8. **Ease:** Only a single variable, the exposure dose/time, must be monitored, making radiation sterilization simple and easy to control.

**Disadvantages of radiation based sterilization:** However, radiation sterilization techniques do have a number of drawbacks:

1. **Instrumentation:** Capital costs are high and specialized facilities are often needed. Gamma radiation requires a nuclear reactor; E-beam/X-ray radiation are generated using electron beam accelerators.
2. **Product Degradation:** Radiation based methods are not compatible with all materials and can cause breakdown of the packaging material and/or product. Common plastics such as polyvinyl chloride (PVC), acetal and polytetrafluoroethylene (PTFE) are sensitive to gamma radiation. The high energies involved in e-beam radiation can also lead to main chain scission (breaking of the long chain backbone) and chemical crosslinking of packaging polymers.
3. **Radioactive material:** When gamma radiation is used as an ionization source, radiation sterilization requires handling and disposal of radioactive material. Note that, at commonly used radiation levels, irradiation with gamma rays does not induce radioactivity in the treated sample itself.

## *3. Autoclave:*

An autoclave is a machine that provides a physical method of sterilization by killing bacteria, viruses, and even spores present in the material put inside of the vessel using steam under pressure.

Autoclave sterilizes the materials by heating them up to a particular temperature for a specific period of time. The autoclave is also called a steam sterilizer that is commonly used in healthcare facilities and industries for various purposes. The autoclave is considered a more effective method of sterilization as it is based on moist heat sterilization.

The simplest form of the autoclave is the pressure cooker type or laboratory bench autoclaves. The following is the detailed description of different components/parts of an autoclave:

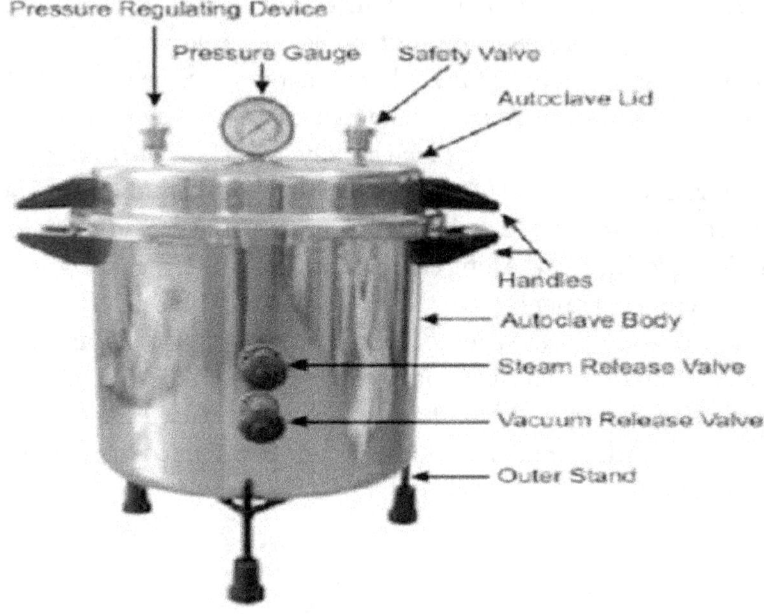


Figure 4: Parts of an Autoclave

**Pressure chamber:** The pressure chamber is the main component of a steam autoclave consisting of an inner chamber and an outer jacket. The inner chamber is made up of stainless steel or gunmetal, which is present inside the out chamber made up of an iron case. The autoclaves used in healthcare laboratories have an outer jacket that is filled with steam to reduce the time taken to reach the sterilization temperature. The inner chamber is the case where the materials to be sterilized are put. The size of the pressure chamber ranges from 100 L to 3000 L.

**Lid/Door:** The next important component of an autoclave is the lid or door of the autoclave. The purpose of the lid is to seal off the outside atmosphere and create a sterilized condition on it inside of the autoclave. The lid is made airtight via the screw clamps and asbestos washer. The lid consists of various other components like:

1. Pressure gauge: A pressure gauge is present on the lid of the autoclave to indicate the pressure created in the autoclave during sterilization. The pressure gauge is essential as it assures the safety of the autoclave and the working condition of the operation.

2. Pressure releasing unit/ Whistle: A whistle is present on the lid of the autoclave is the same as that of the pressure cooker. The whistle controls the pressure inside the chamber by releasing a certain amount of vapour by lifting itself.

3. Safety valve: A safety valve is present on the lid of the autoclave, which is crucial in cases where the autoclave fails to perform its action or the pressure inside increases uncontrollably. The valve has a thin layer of rubber that bursts itself to release the pressure and to avoid the danger of explosion.

**Steam generator/Electrical heater:** An electrical steam generator or boiler is present underneath the chamber that uses an electric heating system to heat the water and generate steam in the inner and the outer chamber. The level of water present in the inner chamber is vital as if the water is not sufficient; there are chances of the burning of the heating system. Similarly, if the water is more than necessary, it might interfere with the tray sand other components present inside the chamber.

**Vacuum generator:** In some types of autoclaves, a separate vacuum generator is present which pulls out the air from the inside of the chamber to create a vacuum inside the chamber. The presence of some air pockets inside the chamber might support the growth of different microorganisms. This is why the vacuum chamber is an important component of an autoclave.

**Wastewater cooler:** Many autoclaves are provided with a system to cool the effluent before it enters the draining pipes. This system prevents any damage to the drainage pipe due to the boiling water being sent out of the autoclave.

The autoclave works on the principle of moist heat sterilization where steam under pressure is used to sterilize the material present inside the chamber. The high pressure increases the boiling point of water and thus helps achieve a higher temperature for sterilization.

Water usually boils at 100°C under normal atmospheric pressure (760 mm of Hg); however, the boiling point of water increases if the pressure is to be increased. Similarly, the high pressure also facilitates the rapid penetration of heat into deeper parts of the material, and moisture present in the steam causes the coagulation of proteins causing an irreversible loss of function and activity of microbes. This principle is employed in an autoclave where the water boils at 121°C at the pressure of 15 psi or 775 mm of Hg.

When this steam comes in contact with the surface, it kills the microbes by giving off latent heat. The condensed liquid ensures the moist killing of the microbes. Once the sterilization phase is completed (which depends on the level of contamination of material inside), the pressure is released from the inside of the chamber through the whistle. The pressure inside the chamber is then restored back to the ambient pressure while the components inside remain hot for some time.

**Advantages & Uses of Autoclave:**

1. An autoclave chamber sterilizes medical or laboratory instruments by heating them above boiling point. Most clinics have table top autoclaves, similar in size to microwave ovens.
2. Hospitals use large autoclaves, also called horizontal autoclaves. They're usually located in the Central Sterile Supply Department (CSSD) and can process numerous surgical instruments in a single sterilization cycle, meeting the ongoing demand for sterile equipment in operating rooms and emergency wards.

**Disadvantages & Uses of Autoclave:**

1. Autoclave is unsuitable for heat sensitive objects. For example, some plastic ware melts in the high heat, and sharp instruments often become dull.
2. Many chemicals breakdown during the sterilization process and oily substances cannot be treated because they do not mix with water.
3. Heating large containers also requires extra time.

# REFERENCES


1. https://medium.com/@aditya.krishna_66867/importance-of-biomaterials-21b3b405e5b9
2. https://www.sciencedirect.com/science/article/pii/B9780128197127000103
3. https://www.sciencedirect.com/topics/materials-science/elastic-moduli
4. https://sist.sathyabama.ac.in/sist_coursematerial/uploads/SBM1304.pdf
5. https://pubmed.ncbi.nlm.nih.gov/33949004/
6. https://www.britannica.com/technology/stainless-steel
7. https://www.americanelements.com/cobalt-chromium-alloy
8. https://www.sciencedirect.com/topics/engineering/titanium-alloys
9. https://www.medicaldesignandoutsourcing.com/what-is-nitinol-and-where-is-it-used/
10. https://www.britannica.com/topic/ceramic-composition-and-properties-103137
11. https://byjus.com/jee/polymerization/
12. https://www.sciencedirect.com/topics/chemistry/polymer-chain
13. https://www.ncbi.nlm.nih.gov/pmc/articles/PMC3136871/
14. https://www.medicalnewstoday.com/articles/248423
15. https://www.health.harvard.edu/staying-healthy/understanding-acute-and-chronic-inflammation
16. https://www.medicalnewstoday.com/articles/196271
17. https://www.sciencedirect.com/topics/medicine-and-dentistry/vascular-graft
18. https://www.ahajournals.org/doi/10.1161/circulationaha.108.778886
19. https://www.mayoclinic.org/tests-procedures/ventricular-assist-device/about/pac-20384529
20. https://www.healthline.com/health/stent
21. https://www.heartandstroke.ca/heart-disease/treatments/surgery-and-other-procedures/implantable-pacemaker
22. https://www.aios.org/cme/cmeseries15.pdf
23. https://monib-health.com/en/post/6-most-common-types-of-orthopedic-implants
24. https://www.hopkinsmedicine.org/health/treatment-tests-and-therapies/knee-replacement-surgery-procedure

25.  https://www.colgate.com/en-in/oral-health/implants/what-are-dental-implants

26.  https://www.yourdentistryguide.com/implants/

27.  https://www.aios.org/cme/cmeseries15.pdf